MHRA STYLE GUIDE

A HANDBOOK FOR
AUTHORS, EDITORS,
AND WRITERS
OF THESES

SECOND EDITION

LONDON
MODERN HUMANITIES RESEARCH ASSOCIATION
2008

This second edition of the *Style Guide* has been edited by a subcommittee of the MHRA consisting of Glanville Price and Brian Richardson (Chairs), Malcolm Cook, Mari Jones, Gerard Lowe, Stephen Parkinson, and Liz Rosindale.

The *Style Guide* may be ordered through the MHRA's website at www.style.mhra.org.uk. It is also available online at this address.

For further information about individual membership and the activities of the MHRA, visit the website at www.mhra.org.uk or contact the Honorary Secretary, Professor David Gillespie, Department of European Studies and Modern Languages, University of Bath, Bath BA2 7AY, UK (email mlsdcg@bath.ac.uk).

ISBN 978-0-947623-76-0

CONTENTS

INTRODUCTION   1

I PREPARING MATERIAL FOR PUBLICATION

1.1   Introduction   2
1.2   General
      1.2.1   Preferred Styles   2
      1.2.2   Electronic Submission   3
      1.2.3   Checking   3
1.3   Preparation of Copy
      1.3.1   General   3
      1.3.2   Instructions for the Typing of Copy
              1.3.2.1   General   4
              1.3.2.2   Corrections, Insertions, and
                        Comments   4
      1.3.3   Fonts and Capitals   5
      1.3.4   Headings and Subdivisions   5
      1.3.5   Dashes   6
      1.3.6   Quotation Marks   6
      1.3.7   Running Heads   6
      1.3.8   Numbering of Pages   7
      1.3.9   Typing Conventions   7
      1.3.10 Special Characters and Diacritics,
              and Non-Latin Scripts   7
      1.3.11 Notes   8
      1.3.12 Illustrations   8
      1.3.13 Tables   10
      1.3.14 Cross-references   10
      1.3.15 Copy Produced on a Typewriter   10
1.4   Author-typeset Formats
      1.4.1   General   11
      1.4.2   Direct Electronic Submission   11

       1.4.3   Camera-ready Copy
              1.4.3.1   General   11
              1.4.3.2   Typographic Style and Layout   11
 1.5   Order of Parts of a Book   12

2   SPELLING AND USAGE

 2.1   Preferred Spellings   14
 2.2   Diacritics   14
 2.3   Hyphens   15
 2.4   Quotations   16
 2.5   Possessives
       2.5.1   General   17
       2.5.2   Proper Names   17
 2.6   Truncations   17
 2.7   Plurals   18

3   NAMES

 3.1   Place-names
       3.1.1   Towns and Cities   19
       3.1.2   Countries   19
 3.2   Academic Institutions   20
 3.3   Personal Names
       3.3.1   Celtic Names   20
       3.3.2   Foreign Names
               3.3.2.1   General   20
              3.3.2.2   Transliteration of Slavonic Names   21

4   ABBREVIATIONS

 4.1   General   23
 4.2   Titles   23
 4.3   In Footnotes and Endnotes   23
 4.4   Use of Full Point   24
 4.5   American States   24

5   PUNCTUATION

 5.1   Commas   25
 5.2   Dashes   26
 5.3   Parentheses and Brackets   27

5.4   Punctuation in Headings   27
5.5   Punctuation with Italics   27
5.6   Quotation Marks   28
5.7   Ellipses and Square Brackets   28

6   CAPITALS

6.1   General   30
6.2   Titles and Dignities   31
6.3   Movements and Periods   31
6.4   Titles of Books and Other Writings   31
6.5   Compounds   33
6.6   Accented Capitals   33
6.7   Small Capitals   34

7   ITALICS

7.1   General   35
7.2   Foreign Words and Quotations   35
7.3   Titles of Books and Other Writings   36
7.4   Titles of Films, Musical Compositions, and
       Works of Art   36

**8   DATES, NUMBERS, CURRENCY, AND WEIGHTS
       AND MEASURES**

8.1   Dates   38
8.2   Numbers   38
8.3   Roman Numerals   39
8.4   Currency   40
8.5   Weights and Measures   41

9   QUOTATIONS AND QUOTATION MARKS

9.1   General   42
9.2   In Languages Other than English   42
9.3   Short Quotations   42
9.4   Long Quotations   44
9.5   Quotations from Plays   45
9.6   Omissions   46
9.7   Copyright and Permissions   46

10 FOOTNOTES AND ENDNOTES

10.1   General   47
10.2   Methods of Limiting Notes   47
10.3   Position and Numbering   47

11 REFERENCES

11.1   General   49
11.2   Forms of Reference
       11.2.1   General   49
       11.2.2   Books   50
       11.2.3   Chapters or Articles in Books   54
       11.2.4   Articles in Journals   56
       11.2.5   Articles in Newspapers and Magazines   58
       11.2.6   Theses and Dissertations   58
       11.2.7   Plays and Long Works   59
       11.2.8   The Bible   59
       11.2.9   Manuscripts   59
       11.2.10 Online Publications
                11.2.10.1   General   60
                11.2.10.2   Online Articles   61
                11.2.10.3   Online Databases   61
                11.2.10.4   Other Sources   62
       11.2.11 Recordings, Films, and Digital Media   62
11.3   Later References   63
11.4   Citation by the Author–Date System   63
11.5   Cross-references   65
11.6   Bibliographies   65

12 PREPARATION OF INDEXES

12.1   General   67
12.2   Index Entries   67
12.3   The Indexer   68

13 PREPARATION OF THESES AND DISSERTATIONS

13.1   General   69
13.2   Length of the Thesis   69

13.3	Parts of the Thesis	
	13.3.1 Title Page	69
	13.3.2 Abstract or Synopsis	70
	13.3.3 Table of Contents and List of Illustrations	70
	13.3.4 Preface, Acknowledgements, Declaration	70
	13.3.5 List of Abbreviations	71
	13.3.6 Text	71
	13.3.7 Notes	71
	13.3.8 Appendices	71
	13.3.9 Bibliography	71
	13.3.10 Index	72
13.4	Preparation of the Typescript	
	13.4.1 General	72
	13.4.2 Headings and Subheadings	72
	13.4.3 Checking and Correction	73
	13.4.4 Cross-references	73
	13.4.5 Illustrations and Tables	73
	13.4.6 Number of Copies	73
13.5	Binding	73
13.6	Permission to Consult and Copy	74
13.7	Further Reading	74

14   USEFUL WORKS OF REFERENCE   75

15   PROOF CORRECTION   76

16   INDEX   87

INTRODUCTION

The *MHRA Style Guide* is intended primarily for use in connection with the Modern Humanities Research Association's own books and periodicals, and with the preparation of theses. However, it is hoped that it will also be widely useful to authors, editors, and publishers.

The *Style Guide* is the successor to the *MHRA Style Book*, first published in 1971 under the editorship of A. S. Maney and R. L. Smallwood, and revised in later editions. This second edition takes account of comments and suggestions made by users of its predecessor, the *Style Guide* of 2002, and we are grateful for these. It has been updated, especially in order to take account of the widespread use of electronic means of text preparation, submission, and publication. Some sections have been revised or expanded for the sake of clarity and completeness, and new ones have been added; in this process, the previous Chapter 2 has been divided into a revised chapter on Spelling and Usage and a new Chapter 3 on Names. Material that seemed redundant has been removed.

Any comments and suggestions for amendments or additions will be welcomed and may be sent to style@mhra.org.uk.

The *Style Guide* is also available online at www.style.mhra.org.uk.

PREPARING MATERIAL FOR PUBLICATION

1.1 INTRODUCTION

This chapter deals with the preparation of copy for editing and subsequent publication in any medium. Many of its principles also hold for the form in which articles are submitted for consideration by journal editors (see 1.2.1). Submission of copy prepared using a word processor is preferred practice, and copy prepared using a typewriter is the exception. Most publishers require authors to supply copy in digital format, usually as an email attachment or on disk. This chapter is therefore written on the assumption that the reader will be using a word processor, although specific guidelines are provided for those using a typewriter (see 1.3.15). In this chapter, 'typed' means 'prepared on a keyboard' (not necessarily on a typewriter) and 'typescript' refers to any form of hard copy produced in this way.

1.2 GENERAL

1.2.1 PREFERRED STYLES

When preparing a text for publication, the author should take due account of the 'Notes for Contributors' or 'Instructions to Authors' of the journal or series. These will specify the form in which articles or book typescripts should be submitted for consideration, and the organization of copy in articles for publication (such as the positioning of abstracts and details of the author's affiliation). While some publications have their own style books or style sheets, most base their 'Notes' on a common guide to style such as this *Style Guide*, with additional specific requirements depending on the preference of their editors, publisher, or printer. Contributors to the MHRA publications *The Slavonic and East European Review* and *The Year's Work in Modern Language Studies* should note that each of these has certain conventions that differ somewhat from those laid down in this *Style Guide*.

If your text incorporates material received from other authors, ensure that it conforms to your own layout.

Once a text has been accepted for publication, editors will normally ask the author to prepare a final revised version of the text, including corrections to the style of the work, in addition to any substantive revisions recommended by readers. As a further safeguard, many publishers employ sub-editors to ensure that final copy is prepared to style before typesetting.

1.2.2 ELECTRONIC SUBMISSION

Always ask your editor what computer file formats, media, and methods of transmission (e.g. disk, email, file upload) are acceptable if this information does not appear in supplied guidelines. The editor will often express a preference for a particular word-processor format (and graphics format where appropriate). If disks are supplied, these should be labelled with the author's name, the title of the work, and the name and details of the version of the software used. Note that although electronic submission is the norm, authors are usually also required to provide a hard-copy printout. The hard copy should correspond exactly to the electronic version.

1.2.3 CHECKING

The final version of copy should be carefully checked before delivery. All quotations should be checked against originals, and not merely against previous drafts of the work. Authors are responsible for the completeness and correctness of references. Ensure that no extraneous comments or queries are embedded in the file. Editors will normally regard the revised version of an article as final and may refuse to accept substantive alterations to proofs or may charge for author corrections.

1.3 PREPARATION OF COPY

1.3.1 GENERAL

The initial submission of an article or monograph will usually be as hard copy only, though an electronic copy may also be required. Editors will circulate the text in this form to readers or referees. In the case of journal articles or conference papers sent anonymously to readers, the author's name will have to be omitted from all pages except the cover page (which the reader will not see). The final form of the text, after all necessary revisions, will normally be supplied electronically and as hard copy. The editors will use the hard copy to indicate minor amendments, to add instructions to the typesetter, and to assess the probable length of the work when made up into printed pages. The typesetter requires a printed version to ensure that all parts of the copy are present in the electronic version and to resolve any problems that may arise when the word-processor file is converted to the typesetter's system. Where special characters or accents or non-Latin scripts are involved, this is essential.

Authors should resist the temptation to overdesign their final copy. The increasing capacity of word processors to manipulate multiple fonts, type sizes, and page layout enables authors to prepare hard copy to a standard matching good typography, but many of these effects are incompatible with typesetters' systems and are lost on conversion. In particular, automatic numbering of lists, headings, and cross-references, in which the word processor fills in the correct number, should be avoided as the codes embedded in the computer files are specific to the word processor and may be lost on conversion. Where authors wish to structure an article into sections, conventional headings (see 1.3.4) should be used. If a specific page layout is required, the hard copy should be annotated accordingly or an explanatory note provided (see 1.3.2.2).

Hard copy should be clearly printed on one side only of good white paper of a standard size, preferably A4 or American letter size. The pages should be numbered (see 1.3.8) and joined with a clip, not stapled. Authors should retain a copy of the submitted version, both on disk and as hard copy.

1.3.2   Instructions for the Typing of Copy

1.3.2.1   general

Double-spacing (to allow for editorial corrections) and one size of a simple typeface should be used throughout, including footnotes or endnotes and extended quotations. Margins of at least 2.5 cm should be left all round and the top quarter of the first page of the text left clear, for a sub-editor's additions. The first line of each paragraph (except the first paragraph of a chapter, section, or article) should be indented by one tab character; do not indent text by inserting multiple spaces. Do not adopt the convention of starting each paragraph full left after an extra line-space; the space between paragraphs should be the normal line spacing. Text should be left-justified but not fully justified. The word processor's automatic hyphenation must be switched off.

Use a serif font such as Times New Roman to avoid confusion of characters such as upper case 'I' and lower case 'l', which can look almost identical in sans serif typefaces such as Arial ('I' and 'l' respectively).

1.3.2.2   corrections, insertions, and comments

Authors should make any corrections to the word-processor file and submit a fully revised version electronically and as hard copy. Editors may need to mark corrections on the hard copy, and, if brief, these should be added legibly in a prominent colour at the appropriate point in the text, so the typesetter can add each emendation to the file efficiently. If a correction consists of more than one or two sentences, or contains typographically complex text, it should be printed on a separate sheet of paper and also supplied electronically, with each word-processor file clearly named and the same convention used for the accompanying hard copy, e.g. 'Insert A'. At the appropriate point in the hard copy of the main text write 'Insert A attached'. Comments for the editor may be made in the margin in pencil or in an accompanying note. Those for the typesetter, to indicate a specific page layout, or the insertion of an illustration (see 1.3.12) or table (see 1.3.13), for example, should be written on the hard copy, encircled, and may be prefaced by either 'TYPESETTER' or 'PRINTER', for clarification, or an explanatory note provided.

1.3.3 FONTS AND CAPITALS

The typesetter will normally have available typefaces in both upper case (large capitals) and lower case, each in roman, italic, and bold versions; in addition, the system should include a typographically separate small capital font. This should not be confused with capital letters printed in a smaller type size since small capital fonts have been separately designed. These alphabets may be seen thus:

LARGE CAPITALS	SMALL CAPITALS	lower case
ITALIC CAPITALS	*ITALIC SMALL CAPITALS*	*italic lower case*
BOLD CAPITALS	**BOLD SMALL CAPITALS**	**bold lower case**

LARGE CAPITALS should be typed as such; text to be set in SMALL CAPITALS should be typed either as such, by using the word processor's small capitals formatting effect, or in lower case with double underlining inserted manually on the hard copy (do not use the word processor's double-underline facility).

For text to be set in italic type (see Chapter 7), authors should use the word processor's italic form of a font, which can be automatically converted. Do not type the copy in roman type and underline it, as was the practice when using a typewriter.

The bold form of a font should not normally be used for emphasis, since it is too obtrusive. However, limited use may be appropriate in some contexts as an alternative to the use of italic, e.g. for highlighting words in the course of lexical analysis.

Ensure that a legible size of font is used so that superior (superscript) and inferior (subscript) figures and diacritical and punctuation marks can be clearly seen.

1.3.4 HEADINGS AND SUBDIVISIONS

Do not type headings or subheadings in capitals and do not underline or italicize them, since either method may conflict with the style which the editor wishes the printer to follow. No punctuation marks (other than question marks) should be used after headings or subheadings.

Major subdivisions within the text, if required, should be marked by increased spacing. The first line of a new subdivision should not be indented.

A convenient system for designating numbered subdivisions is to number all sections and subsections with arabic numerals and express them in series, divided by full points, as in this *Style Guide*.

1.3.5   DASHES

For discussion of usage, see 5.2. Although word processors have the facility to indicate the short dash or en rule (–), the long dash or em rule (—), and the extended dash or 2-em rule (——), the following practice is recommended:

- An en rule in numerical spans should be represented by a hyphen with no space on either side
- An en rule linking two lexical items should be represented by two hyphens with no space on either side
- An em rule should be represented by two hyphens with space on either side
- A 2-em rule should be represented by three unspaced hyphens

According to these principles, the examples of usage given in the left-hand column will be typed as in the right-hand column:

the 1939–45 war	the 1939-45 war
the north–south divide	the north--south divide
Some people — an ever increasing number — deplore this	Some people -- an ever increasing number -- deplore this
Brontë, Charlotte, *Shirley* —— *Villette*	Brontë, Charlotte, *Shirley* --- *Villette*

1.3.6   QUOTATION MARKS

Many word processors will automatically convert straight single and double quotation marks to 'smart quotes' (' ' and " "), and this function should be used when preparing copy for the printer. If this feature is not available, type a backward-slanting mark (`) to open single quotes and a vertical mark (') to close single quotes, and for double quotation marks type these single quotation marks twice.

1.3.7   RUNNING HEADS

Shortened headings may be required at the heads of printed pages after the first page of the article or chapter. A preferred abbreviated version of the title could be provided by the author on submission of copy and indicated at the top of the first page of the hard copy.

1.3.8 NUMBERING OF PAGES

Ensure that all pages of the hard copy (including notes or references) are numbered consecutively in the top right-hand corner, and indicate the total number of pages on the first page. If any pages are added or removed during revision, the entire printed copy must be renumbered.

1.3.9 TYPING CONVENTIONS

The basic formatting of the text, particularly the division into pages and lines, should be left to the typesetter. In particular, do not use any of the ad hoc formatting devices available on your word processor, such as manual page breaks and variations of page dimensions, to fit text neatly on whole pages. This may detract from the visual aspect of your final copy, but it will avoid any need for the typesetter to change the format of your copy before it can be processed. Use hyphens only as recommended in 2.3; do not use automatic hyphenation. The return key (or paragraph marker) should be used only at the end of paragraphs and headings, or to divide the lines of tables, lists, or verse quotations.

Double spaces should not be used in normal text, and should be eliminated from your copy before submission. In particular, type only a single space between the end of a sentence and the first character of the next, and following major punctuation marks such as colons and semicolons.

Do not right justify or centre any parts of the text, as this will introduce additional spaces which are not easily distinguished from typed spaces. Do not use coloured backgrounds to highlight text.

1.3.10 SPECIAL CHARACTERS AND DIACRITICS, AND NON-LATIN SCRIPTS

If your text contains characters that are not directly available from a standard computer keyboard, you should consult the editor or publisher as to the best way to insert them in your copy. The special character sets provided by major word processors are acceptable to many publishers; devices for creating and combining characters should be avoided. When your text contains special characters or diacritics identified as problematic, highlight the first instance on the hard copy, and indicate in the margin the word-processor character or string of characters used to obtain them. Some publishers specify codes for non-standard characters. In extreme cases, special characters may be indicated by hand on the hard copy, or represented by specially devised codes, with appropriate indications in the margin. Where your text contains a significant number of special characters, it is advisable to list them all on a separate sheet of paper, for submission along with the final copy.

Alphabets such as Cyrillic and Greek and the International Phonetic Alphabet (IPA) may cause conversion problems for typesetters, who can suggest a specific method of producing the copy (e.g. through the use of Unicode-based fonts). For transliteration of Cyrillic characters, see 3.3.2.2. Additional problems arise with other alphabetic scripts (such as Arabic and Hebrew) and non-alphabetic scripts (such as Chinese and Japanese). In all such cases, consult the editor at an early stage.

The following publications contain much useful information on copy preparation and typesetting for languages other than English, both those using the Latin alphabet and others:

> *New Oxford Dictionary for Writers and Editors* (Oxford: Oxford University Press, 2005)
> *The Chicago Manual of Style*, 15th edn (Chicago and London: University of Chicago Press, 2003)

1.3.11   NOTES

Footnote or endnote reference numbers should be inserted following any punctuation except a dash, and at the end of a sentence if possible:

> [...] composed.[23]

Many typesetting programs are able to convert the standard footnoting and endnoting facilities of a word processor, but it is recommended that authors check the guidelines for authors provided by the publication, or discuss the use of these facilities with the editor or publisher, before preparing an article or book for submission. Where these facilities are unavailable or should not be used, notes should be supplied in a separate file, with reference numbers typed as superior (superscript) figures in the appropriate place.

The notes will normally be set in type smaller than that used for the text but should be provided by the author in full type size with double spacing (whether generated from a word-processor noting facility or supplied as a separate text file) and numbered consecutively throughout an article or chapter, but not throughout a whole book or thesis.

1.3.12   ILLUSTRATIONS

The inclusion of any illustrative material should always be discussed with the editor prior to submission. For all illustrations that are in copyright, the author must obtain, from all interested rightsholders, written permission to reproduce in all publication formats (print or electronic), including confirmation of the credit to be printed acknowledging permission to reproduce. Top copies of permission documents should be supplied with the illustrations. The responsibility for payment of costs for reproduction should also be discussed with the editor at an early stage.

Increasingly, illustrations can be supplied electronically and for most typesetters this will be the preferred format. The appropriate resolution, file format, and means of submission should be discussed with the editor. It is recommended that TIFF or EPS files should be supplied, saved at a minimum input scanning resolution of 300 dpi (dots-per-inch) for colour, 350–400 dpi for halftones, 800 dpi for simple line, and 1200 dpi for fine line images. JPEG images are usually not recommended for printing purposes, unless files are available at print-quality resolutions. All illustrations should be supplied as separate files, not embedded within the text, with accompanying hard copy for reference.

Where illustrations are not available in electronic format, a clear original in black ink on white paper or board for line illustrations, and glossy black-and-white photographs for halftones, should be provided. For all illustrations indicate clearly on the reverse the title of the book or journal, the author's name, and the figure or plate number. Be careful to write very lightly in pencil on the reverse of an original or it may be spoiled. Some reduction may improve definition, but excessive reduction may cause detail, such as fine lines or close shading, to be lost. Normally the original should not be more than four times larger, nor should it be smaller, than the final required size of the image. A general indication of the preferred size of reproduction, e.g. 'half page', 'text width', along with specific groupings, e.g. 'figures 1 and 2 on same page', should be given in an accompanying note as a guideline for the typesetter. If part of the illustration is to be omitted, indicate on an accompanying photocopy the portion to be masked off. Where this is not possible, indicate lightly on the reverse of the original or on an attached paper overlay.

The style for referencing an illustration within the text should be ascertained from the editor or guidelines for authors but is generally by insertion of the phrase 'Figure [...]'. A reference is necessary because an illustration is unlikely to follow the relevant text immediately, for technical reasons. A note 'Figure [...] here' should be added to the margin of the hard copy as a guide for the typesetter. Figures should be numbered in sequence in arabic numerals throughout an article or book.

The term 'plate' is applicable only to pages of illustrations printed, and numbered, separately from the text; it refers to the page, not to the illustrations on it (so one plate may contain more than one illustration). Plates should be numbered in sequence in roman numerals and a reference given within the text ('Plate [...]').

Authors who are not sure of the intended treatment of their illustrations should consult the editor before numbering them.

Captions for illustrations should be supplied as a separate file with accompanying hard copy. Acknowledgement of permission to reproduce the illustration, where appropriate, should be indicated below the caption.

1.3.13   TABLES

Tables may not always convert satisfactorily from word-processed files. They should be prepared using the word processor's standard table routine if possible, but, if not, columns should be separated by standard tabulation. They should not be embedded within the text but should be either placed at the end of the text or supplied as separate files, with accompanying hard copy. A reference to the table should be included within the text at an appropriate point ('Table [...]'), as, for technical reasons, it may not be possible for the table to be printed immediately following the relevant text. A note 'Table [...] here' should be added to the margin of the hard copy as a guide for the typesetter. Tables should be numbered in sequence in arabic numerals throughout an article, book, or thesis.

1.3.14   CROSS-REFERENCES

Since they cannot be finalized until the text is typeset, cross-references within an article or book should be typed as zeros on the hard copy and encircled in ink:

See above [or below], p.⟨ooo⟩ n.⟨o⟩

Internal cross-referencing, i.e. cross-references to pages within your own document, should be avoided as far as possible; it is preferable to cross-refer to chapters, sections, notes, etc. Where internal cross-referencing to a page is unavoidable, the relevant page number in the hard copy should be noted in pencil in the margin and such cross-references should be carefully checked and marked on the proofs.

1.3.15   COPY PRODUCED ON A TYPEWRITER

Whilst many electronic typewriters can produce effects such as underlining, it is difficult to produce the same formatting as on a word processor.

Text to be set in a particular font should be marked (manually if necessary) as follows:

- Italic text to be underlined once
- Small capitals to be underlined twice
- Capitals to be typed in capitals, or typed in lower case and underlined three times
- Italic capitals to be typed as capitals and underlined once.

See Chapter 15, 'Proof Correction', for an illustration of these conventions.

1.4   AUTHOR-TYPESET FORMATS

1.4.1   GENERAL

Where economy or speed is an important concern, an author may be asked to prepare typeset pages in the final form in which they are to be published. This may apply to entire monographs or to items in newsletters or collections or preprints of conference papers. The author should be guided by the instructions of the volume or series editor on issues of style, usage, and formatting, to ensure consistency within the volume and between volumes. For MHRA volumes prepared by this means, authors should follow this *Style Guide.*

1.4.2   DIRECT ELECTRONIC SUBMISSION

Sophisticated word-processing and desktop publishing (DTP) software allows authors to submit their content digitally as made-up pages. This may take the form of files in the format of the program used, or PostScript or PDF files, which are used by the printer to produce printing plates. As always, it is essential to consult the printer about file formats and methods of transferring files before beginning work, and authors should still have regard to matters of style and layout as mentioned in 1.4.3.2 below.

1.4.3   CAMERA-READY COPY

1.4.3.1   GENERAL

The term camera-ready copy (CRC) was originally used to describe a printed copy of the text on single pages that is used for the production of film and printing plates without further intervention by editor or printer, but it is also now commonly used to describe electronic files that are supplied as made-up pages ready for press. Whether electronic files or paper are to be supplied, it is essential to consult the printer about requirements for the preparation of copy before beginning work.

1.4.3.2   TYPOGRAPHIC STYLE AND LAYOUT

Printers will often now provide word-processor style/template documents for authors to use in preparing manuscripts. These documents follow the printer's typographical styling and layout requirements and PDF or PostScript files can be produced from them. Where printed CRC is required, it should be noted that copy is commonly prepared using a page size larger than the final printed size, so that it can be reduced and the density of the type increased. Consistent guidelines should be drawn up, especially if a volume prepared in this way is to form one of a series. These may include a grid specifying the width and depth of the text area; the position of running heads and page numbers relative to the text and their location on an A4 page; a specified typeface; type sizes for text, quotations, notes, etc., capable of reduction in scale without loss of legibility; style of chapter titles and headings; and rules on word breaks and line and page ends.

CRC should be printed on high-quality white paper, using a laser printer, and to the highest resolution in terms of dots-per-inch (dpi) possible. All parts of the work should be presented in the correct order (see 1.5 below), each page being printed on one side only.

1.5　　ORDER OF PARTS OF A BOOK

Before submission to editor or publisher, the text of a book should be arranged in the order listed below. Authors undertaking the typesetting of a book, whether as DTP or by CRC, should have regard to this list, and to which pages (generally preliminaries) may be conventionally typeset in a series with standing matter or an established format.

The typescript of a book should be arranged in the order requested by the publisher. The following order is preferred for MHRA publications:

Half-title (the full title, including any subtitle, of the book, and the title of the series and the volume number in that series, if applicable; the name of the author does not normally appear); the verso of this page is usually left blank when the book is printed or may carry a frontispiece
Title page
Bibliographical details (name and address of the publisher and printer, copyright statement, International Standard Book Number (ISBN), Cataloguing-in-Publication Data, etc.); this page may be left blank by the author and the details supplied by the editor and publisher
Dedication or epigraph (the verso is left blank)
Contents list
List of illustrations (figures, maps, plates, in that order)
Foreword (by someone other than the author)
Author's preface
Acknowledgements (if not included in the author's preface)
List of abbreviations and/or glossary if these are necessary to an understanding of the text; otherwise they may be placed towards the end of the book, before the bibliography
Introduction (unless this constitutes the first chapter of the text)
Text
Appendix or appendices
Notes and references (for the whole text)
Bibliography
Index or indexes

Few books will include everything listed above; some items may be requested at a late stage in production.

The copyright should be indicated thus: international copyright symbol (©); name of holder of copyright; year of first publication. The printer's name and usual place of business must appear on the first or last leaf of the publication and may conveniently be combined with the publisher's imprint. The preliminary pages ('prelims'), comprising all items before the main text, are usually numbered in lower-case roman numerals; though these numbers are not printed on certain pages (half-title, title, etc.), they are counted in the sequence. Arabic numbering usually begins on the first page of the text. However, since the page numbers cannot be added by the printer until the page proofs are prepared, all the pages of the typescript should be numbered in one (arabic) sequence throughout (see 1.3.8).

SPELLING AND USAGE

2.1   PREFERRED SPELLINGS

In the case of verbs ending in *-ize* or *-ise* and their derivatives, the forms in *-ize, -ization*, etc. (e.g. *civilize, civilization*) are preferred in MHRA publications. This is also the preferred spelling of many other academic publishers. However, all major British newspapers and most official and commercial bodies prefer *-ise, -isation*. It is important, within a given book or article, to be consistent.

Some words must have the *-ise* spelling, e.g.:

advertise	comprise	devise	franchise	supervise
advise	compromise	enterprise	improvise	surmise
apprise	demise	excise	incise	surprise
chastise	despise	exercise	revise	televise

The British spelling of *analyse* and its derivatives has *s* and not *z*.

The forms *disk, program* are used even in British spelling in computing contexts; otherwise, use *disc, programme*.

In case of doubt, the form given in the *New Oxford Dictionary for Writers and Editors* should in most cases be used (but for diacritics, see 2.2).

2.2   DIACRITICS

There is great inconsistency between dictionaries (and sometimes within the same dictionary) as to the use of accents and other diacritics in words borrowed from other languages.

Two cases are, however, clear:

(a) When a word or, more often, an expression is still felt to be foreign (and an objective decision is not always possible), all diacritics should be retained, e.g.:

aide-mémoire, ancien régime, à la mode, Aufklärung, la belle époque, bête noire, cause célèbre, déjà vu, éminence grise, Führer, lycée, maître d'hôtel, papier mâché, pièce de résistance, più, raison d'être, señor, succès de scandale, tête-à-tête

Such words and expressions are often italicized (see also 7.2).

(b) Words ending in -*é* retain their accent:

blasé, café, cliché, communiqué, exposé, fiancé (also fiancée)

In such words, any other accents are also retained, e.g.:

émigré, pâté, protégé, résumé

We recommend that, except as provided for in (b) above, diacritics should be dropped in the case of words that have passed into regular English usage, e.g.:

chateau, cortege, creche, crepe, debacle, debris, decor, denouement, detente, echelon, elite, fete, hotel, matinee, naive, precis, premiere, regime, role, seance, soiree

For the use of accents on capitals, see 6.6.

2.3 HYPHENS

Hyphens should be used only when they have a specific purpose. They occasionally occur within the body of a word, particularly with *re-* followed by *e* (e.g. *re-echo, re-enter*), but they normally indicate that two or more words are to be read as a single word with only one main stress. The examples given below show forms that are attributive and have a single main stress and are therefore hyphenated, while predicative and other forms having two main stresses are not hyphenated:

a well-known fact	the facts are well known
a tenth-century manuscript	in the tenth century

Nevertheless, to avoid a proliferation of hyphens and where there is no possibility of ambiguity, forms such as *a late eighteenth-century novelist, post-Second World War difficulties*, are to be preferred to *a late-eighteenth-century novelist, post-Second-World-War difficulties*.

In phrases such as *pre- and post-war governments, pro- and anti-abortion movements, eighteenth- and nineteenth-century literature*, where two or more parallel hyphenated terms are combined, the first hyphen is followed by a space.

Adverbs ending in *-ly* and other polysyllabic adverbs are not hyphenated to a following adjective or participle:

a highly contentious argument
a recently published novel
a handsomely bound volume
a frequently occurring mistake
a hitherto unrecognized custom
ever increasing quantities

Collocations of certain monosyllabic adverbs (in particular *ill* but not *well* —
see above) and a participle often have only one main stress and are therefore
hyphenated even when used predicatively:

> He is very ill-tempered.
> Such a course of action would be ill-advised.
> These prejudices are deep-seated.

Note that, unlike the words *early*, *late*, *north*, *south*, etc., the prefix *mid-*
always requires a hyphen (except where it forms part of a single word, as in
midnight):

> The boat sank in mid-Atlantic.
> a mid-June midnight flight
> a mid-sixteenth-century chair
> until the mid-nineteenth century

The presence or absence of a hyphen is often significant:

> two-year-old dogs   two year-old dogs
> a deep-blue lake   a deep blue lake
> a vice-chancellor   the vice squad
> to re-cover   to recover

Usage shifts over time and forms that were once entirely acceptable may
now seem odd or old-fashioned. Some words that used to be hyphenated
have now become so common that they are regarded as single unhyphenated
words:

> battlefield, bookshelf, paperback, subcommittee, subtitle

In short, if a compound is in frequent use and is pronounced as a single
word it is usually acceptable to write it as one word without a hyphen. There
is considerable variation in the use of hyphens and it is impossible to formulate
comprehensive rules. The best advice is to use a good dictionary and to be
consistent.

2.4   QUOTATIONS

The spelling of quotations is always that of the book or edition referred
to. Note, however, that in quotations from early printed books the forms of
the letters *i* and *j*, *u* and *v*, the long *s* (ſ or *f*) the ampersand (&), the Tironian
sign (7), the tilde, superior (superscript) letters in contractions, and other
abbreviations are normalized to modern usage unless there are good reasons
to the contrary, as, for example, in full bibliographical descriptions.

2.5 POSSESSIVES

2.5.1 GENERAL

The possessive of nouns and indefinite pronouns is regularly formed by the addition of *s* preceded by the apostrophe:

the court's decision, the doctor's fee, the boss's daughter, Smith's elixir, no one's fault, the children's day out

The possessive forms of personal pronouns *hers, its, theirs, yours* do not have an apostrophe.

In plural nouns ending in -*s* the possessive is represented by the apostrophe alone:

the courts' decisions, the doctors' fees, the bosses' daughters, MPs' assistants

2.5.2 PROPER NAMES

The possessive of proper names ending in a pronounced -*s* or -*z* is formed in the normal way by adding an apostrophe and *s*:

Alvarez's criticism, Berlioz's symphonies, Cervantes's works, Dickens's characters, in Inigo Jones's day, Keats's poems, Dylan Thomas's use of language

French names ending in an unpronounced -*s*, -*x*, or -*z* also follow the normal rule and take an apostrophe and *s*:

Rabelais's comedy, Descartes's works, Malraux's style, Cherbuliez's novels

The possessive of names ending in -*us* also conforms to the normal rule:

Claudius's successor, Herodotus's *Histories*, Jesus's parables, an empire greater than Darius's

However, the possessive of *Moses* and of Greek names ending in -*es* (particularly those having more than two syllables) is usually formed by means of the apostrophe alone:

under Moses' leadership, Demosthenes' speeches, Sophocles' plays, Xerxes' campaigns

2.6 TRUNCATIONS

Some words are abbreviated by omitting the first part of the word. If such abbreviations are in common use, no apostrophe is needed:

bus (*not* 'bus); phone (*not* 'phone); the twenties (i.e. 1920s) (*not* 'twenties)

2.7   PLURALS

Some nouns borrowed from foreign languages have only the regular English plural, e.g.:

> (Greek) metropolis, metropolises
>
> (Latin) campus, campuses; census, censuses; album, albums; forum, forums; museum, museums; premium, premiums
>
> (Italian) canto, cantos; libretto, librettos; soprano, sopranos; sonata, sonatas

Some nouns, especially ones adopted from Greek and Latin, have only the foreign plural ending, e.g.:

> (Greek) analysis, analyses; axis, axes; basis, bases; crisis, crises; diagnosis, diagnoses; oasis, oases; thesis, theses (and similarly with hypothesis, parenthesis, synthesis); criterion, criteria; phenomenon, phenomena
>
> (Latin) alumnus, alumni; stimulus, stimuli; addendum, addenda; datum, data; desideratum, desiderata; erratum, errata; codex, codices
>
> (German) lied, lieder

Other borrowed nouns may have either the English or the foreign plural. In general, the foreign plural is less common and more formal, or it may have a more specialized sense, as in these words of Greek or Latin origin:

> formula (formulas in everyday usage, formulae in mathematics); thesaurus (thesauruses, thesauri); medium (mediums in spiritualism, media for (plural) means of communication); memorandum (memorandums, memoranda); referendum (referendums, referenda); ultimatum (ultimatums, ultimata); corpus (corpuses, corpora); appendix (appendixes for parts of the body, appendixes or appendices for additional parts of a publication); index (indexes for alphabetical lists of references, indices in mathematics)

Some adopted French words may retain the original plural -*x*, but -*s* is also found:

> adieu (adieus, adieux); milieu (milieus, milieux); tableau (tableaus, tableaux)

See also 8.4 on the plurals of foreign currencies.

No apostrophe should be used before the plural ending of abbreviations (where the -*s* follows any punctuation), names, numbers, letters, and words not normally used as nouns, e.g.:

> MPs, POWs, Ph.D.s
> the Henrys, the two Germanys
> the 1960s, the twenties, ones and twos
> *a*s and *e*s, the three Rs
> haves and have nots

NAMES

3.1 PLACE-NAMES

3.1.1 TOWNS AND CITIES

Where there is a current English form for foreign names of towns or cities (e.g. *Basle, Cologne, Dunkirk, Florence, Geneva, Lisbon, Majorca, Moscow, Munich, Naples, Quebec, Salonika, Venice, Vienna*), it should be used. Obsolete English forms (*Francfort, Leipsic, Leghorn*, etc.) should, however, be avoided. The forms *Luxembourg, Lyon, Marseille, Reims*, and *Strasbourg* are now more widely used than *Luxemburg, Lyons, Marseilles, Rheims*, and *Strasburg* or *Strassburg* and are therefore recommended.

The following are now the official spellings of certain Welsh names (even in texts written in English) and should be used instead of the anglicized forms found in earlier maps and in earlier books: *Aberdyfi, Aberystwyth, Betws-y-Coed, Caernarfon, Conwy* (river and town), *Dolgellau, Ffestiniog, Llanelli, Tywyn*.

The use or non-use of hyphens in names such as *Newcastle upon Tyne, Stratford-upon-Avon* should be checked in a good reference work. French place-names are regularly hyphenated, e.g. *Colombey-les-Deux-Églises, Châlons-sur-Marne, Saint-Malo*, except for an introductory definite article, e.g. *Le Havre, Les Baux-de-Provence*.

Note the correct form of the name of *Washington, DC* (comma, no stops).

For forms of reference to the place of publication of books, see 11.2.2 and 11.6.

3.1.2 COUNTRIES

Distinguish between (a) Great Britain (i.e. England, Scotland, Wales), (b) the United Kingdom (England, Scotland, Wales, Northern Ireland), (c) the British Isles (England, Scotland, Wales, Ireland, the Isle of Man, the Channel Islands).

Note:
(a) that *England* should never be used for any of the above;
(b) that the term *Britain* in its strict sense is the equivalent of *Great Britain* but is so extensively used as the equivalent of *the United Kingdom* that it would be pedantic to object to its use in that sense;
(c) that the Irish form *Éire* should not be used in English as the name of the Republic of Ireland;
(d) that the Isle of Man and the Channel Islands are not parts of England, of Great Britain, or of the United Kingdom.

The definite article is no longer used in the names of the countries *Lebanon, Sudan*, and *Ukraine* (but *the Gambia, the Netherlands*).

3.2 ACADEMIC INSTITUTIONS

Care needs to be taken to ensure that the names of academic institutions are correctly given, e.g. *Johns Hopkins University* (not *John*), *Magdalen College* (Oxford), *Magdalene College* (Cambridge). Universities and colleges with similar names must be clearly distinguished, such as the University of California and California State University, the University of York (England) and York University (Toronto).

3.3 PERSONAL NAMES

3.3.1 CELTIC NAMES

Care must be taken over the spelling of names in *Mc, Mac*, etc. (e.g. *McDonald, MacDonald, M'Donald, Macmillan, Mac Liammóir*); adopt the form used by the individual in question. All such forms, whatever the spelling adopted, are alphabetized as if they began with *Mac*.

Likewise, distinguish between Irish names that retain their original form (*Ó Máille*) and those that are anglicized (*O'Donnell*).

Welsh names in *ap* and *ab* are neither capitalized nor hyphenated. Names of historical figures are alphabetized under the first name (e.g. *Dafydd ap Gwilym, Dafydd ab Owain*), modern names under *ap* or *ab* (e.g. *ap Gwilym, ab Owen Edwards*).

3.3.2 FOREIGN NAMES

3.3.2.1 GENERAL

Where generally accepted English forms of classical names exist (*Horace, Livy, Ptolemy, Virgil*), they should be used.

Names of popes and saints should normally be given in their English form (*Gregory, Innocent, Paul, St Francis of Assisi, St John of the Cross, St Thomas Aquinas*).

Names of foreign kings and queens should normally be given in their English form where one exists (*Charles V, Catherine the Great, Ferdinand and Isabella, Francis I, Henry IV, Victor Emmanuel*). Those names for which no English form exists (*Haakon, Sancho*) or for which the English form is quaint or archaic (*Alphonse, Lewis* for *Alfonso, Louis*) should retain their foreign form. If in the course of a work it is necessary to refer to some monarchs whose names have acceptable English forms and some which do not, in the interests of consistency it is better to use the foreign form for all:

the reigns of Fernando III and Alfonso X
Henri IV was succeeded by Louis XIII.

Surnames in *van* take a lower case initial in the Netherlands (*van der Plas, van Toorn*) but are generally capitalized in Belgium (*Van den Bremt, Van Ryssel*).

With reference to the Prophet, use the form *Muhammad* and not *Mohammed* or *Mahomet*. Likewise, *Muslim* not *Moslem* or *Mohammedan, Muhammadan*, etc.

3.3.2.2 TRANSLITERATION OF SLAVONIC NAMES

Various systems exist for the transliteration of Russian and other languages using the Cyrillic alphabet. Contributors to journals, series, etc. in the field of Slavonic studies should ascertain which system is preferred and conform to it strictly. The MHRA specifies that the Library of Congress system without diacritics is to be used in all its publications in the Slavonic field, namely *The Slavonic and East European Review*, the Slavonic article and review sections of *The Modern Language Review*, the Slavonic sections of *The Year's Work in Modern Language Studies*, and relevant volumes in the Publications of the MHRA, MHRA Texts and Dissertations, and MHRA Bibliographies series. Thus for instance:

Dostoevskii, Chaikovskii, Tolstoi, Evtushenko

Russian and other Slavonic names referred to in other contexts should, wherever possible, be given in the form recommended by the *New Oxford Dictionary for Writers and Editors*, even when this conflicts with the Library of Congress system:

Dostoevsky, Tchaikovsky, Tolstoy, Yevtushenko

Note in particular that, except in the one case of Tchaikovsky, Ch- not Tch-should be used (e.g. Chekhov) and that the prime (′) should not be used:

Gogol, Gorky, Ilya (*compare* Library of Congress: Gogol′, Gor′kii, Il′ia).

4 ABBREVIATIONS

4.1 GENERAL

Since abbreviations increase the possibility of confusion and misunderstanding, they should be used with caution. When writing for a particular publication, use only those abbreviations which are likely to be familiar to its readers. Never begin a sentence with an abbreviation, and avoid abbreviations as far as possible in passages of continuous prose. For example:

> The author's comments on page 47, line 20, seem particularly apt.

Here the words 'page' and 'line', normally abbreviated in references, are given in full to prevent a disruptive effect in reading. Extensively used abbreviations, other than common ones like 'p.' and 'l.', should be clearly listed at the beginning of a book or in an early note to an article.

4.2 TITLES

Avoid inelegant or confusing abbreviations of the titles of literary works, especially in the text of your book or article. It is clearly necessary to avoid frequent repetition of a title, especially a long one, and discreet abbreviation will from time to time be needed. This should normally take the form of a short title, not initials: *All's Well*, not *AWEW*. Repetition can often be avoided in other ways: e.g. 'the play', when it is obvious which play is meant. In notes, and in parenthetical textual references in the main body of a book or article, abbreviations are more often appropriate, but they need not be inelegant and must never confuse. Note, however, that abbreviated titles are standard in some cultures, e.g. *PMC* for *Poema de mio Cid*. See 10.2 on the avoidance of repeated note references to the same work.

4.3 IN FOOTNOTES AND ENDNOTES

If possible, do not begin a note with an abbreviation which is normally printed in lower-case characters ('e.g.', 'i.e.', 'pp.'). If this cannot be avoided, note that '*c.*', 'e.g.', 'i.e.', 'l.', 'll.', 'p.', 'pp.', remain entirely in lower case:

> [21] pp. 127–39. *not* [21] Pp. 127–39.

Other abbreviations, such as 'Cf.', 'Ibid.', or 'Id.', take a capital initial.

4.4   USE OF FULL POINT

A contracted form of a word that ends with the same letter as the full form, including plural -*s*, is not followed by a full point:

> Dr, Jr, Mme, Mr, Mrs, St, vols

but note the exception 'no.' for Italian 'numero'. Other abbreviations take a full point and are followed by a space:

> M. Dupont (Monsieur), Prof. J. Jones, l. 6, ll. 22–28, p. 6, pp. 106–09, vol. XIX

In lower-case abbreviations for expressions consisting of more than one word, there is a full point after each initial:

> a.m. (*ante meridiem*), e.g. (*exempli gratia*), i.e. (*id est*), n.p. (no place [of publication]), n.d. (no date [of publication])

Full points are omitted in capitalized abbreviations or acronyms for:

(a) standard works of reference (italicized), journals (italicized), or series (not italicized):

> *DNB, OED, ABELL, MLR, PMLA, TLS*, BAR, PMHRS, PRF, TBL

(b) countries, institutions, societies, and organizations (none of them italicized):

> UK, USA, BL, BM, UNAM, CNRS, ANTS, MHRA, MLA, UNESCO

In bibliographical references, use MS, MSS ('manuscript(s)'). In normal prose text the word should be written out in full.

4.5   AMERICAN STATES

The two-letter postal abbreviations for American states, e.g.:

> CA (California), IL (Illinois), MA (Massachusetts), NY (New York)

have largely replaced the official abbreviations, though a few of these, in particular 'Calif.' and 'Mass.', are still widely used. The postal abbreviations, which have no full point, should be used whenever it is necessary to include the name of the state in bibliographical references (11.2.2, list of items, no. 7). These abbreviations are given in the *New Oxford Dictionary for Writers and Editors*.

5 PUNCTUATION

5.1 COMMAS

Commas are used singly or in pairs to indicate significant groupings or separations of words in the sentence. Particular note should be taken of the following usages:

a) Commas should be used to delimit parenthetical or interpolated phrases, and nouns in apposition:

> My father, not to mention the rest of my family, felt the loss deeply.
>
> This book, written in 1505, would change the world.
>
> Dante, the Florentine poet, was born in 1265.

Note that a noun preceded by a defining phrase is not in apposition and should not be enclosed in commas:

> The Florentine poet Dante was born in 1265.

b) Commas are used to delimit *non-restrictive* relative clauses, which do not define what precedes:

> Those with a university degree, who have experience of higher education, see qualifications in a different light.
>
> The family had two cats, which slept indoors, and a dog.

No commas are used in the corresponding *restrictive* relative clauses:

> Those with a university degree who have studied medicine see research in a different light.
>
> The family had two cats which slept indoors and one which went out at night.

c) In an enumeration of three or more items, it is the preferred style in MHRA publications to insert commas after all but the last item, to give equal weight to each enumerated element:

> The University has departments of French, German, Spanish, and Portuguese within its Faculty of Arts.

The conjunctions *and* and *or* without a preceding comma are understood as linking the parts of a single enumerated element:

> The University has departments of French, German, Spanish and Portuguese, Czech and Polish, and Dutch.

> Comedians such as Laurel and Hardy, Abbott and Costello, or Charlie Chaplin

By the same principle a comma should be used before a phrase such as 'and so on' or 'etc.' at the end of an enumeration.

d) Commas should not be used if their omission leaves the meaning of the sentence unaffected. The mere fact that a sentence has a complex subject does not justify the use of a comma between the subject and verb. Accordingly a sentence like

> The team of editors responsible for the latest edition of the handbook has made a significant number of changes.

requires no comma following 'handbook'.

5.2   DASHES

Printers use both a short and a long dash.

The short dash ('en rule') is used to indicate a span or a differentiation and may be considered as a substitute for 'and' or 'to' (but see 8.1):

> the England–France match; the 1939–45 war; pp. 81–101

Long dashes ('em rules'), often with a space on either side, are normally found in pairs to enclose parenthetical statements, or singly to denote a break in the sentence:

> Some people — an ever increasing number — deplore this.

> Family and fortune, health and happiness — all were gone.

Long dashes should be used sparingly; commas, colons, or parentheses are often more appropriate. Other punctuation marks should not normally be used before or after a dash.

A very long dash (——), known as a '2-em dash', is used to indicate 'ditto' in bibliographies and similar lists:

> Marlowe, Christopher, *Edward II*
> —— *The Jew of Malta*

For means of representing the different dashes in typescript, see 1.3.5.

5.3   PARENTHESES AND BRACKETS

In its strict sense, the term 'brackets' means 'square brackets', i.e. [ ], and should not be used with reference to parentheses, i.e. ( ). However, since it is widely misused, it is as well always to specify 'square brackets', 'round brackets' (or 'parentheses'), 'angle brackets', i.e. < >, or 'braces', i.e. { }, and avoid the use of the term 'brackets' alone.

Parentheses are used for parenthetical statements and references within a text. When a passage within parentheses falls at the end of a sentence of which it is only a part, the final full point is placed outside the closing parenthesis:

> This was well reviewed at the time (for instance in *TLS*, 9 July 1971, p. 817).

When a complete sentence is within parentheses, the final full point should be inside the closing parenthesis. Parentheses may be used within parentheses:

> (His presidential address (1967) made this point clearly.)

Square brackets should be used for the enclosure of phrases or words which have been added to the original text or for editorial and similar comments:

> He adds that 'the lady [Mrs Jervis] had suffered great misfortunes'.
>
> I do not think they should have [*two words illegible*].
>
> He swore to tell the truth, the old [*sic*] truth, and nothing but the truth.

For the use of brackets around ellipses, see 5.7. For the use of brackets in references to the publication of books, see 11.2.2.

5.4   PUNCTUATION IN HEADINGS

Punctuation marks (other than question marks) should not be used at the end of headings and subheadings. Punctuation marks should also be omitted after items in lists which are in tabular form (except, of course, full points used to mark abbreviations).

5.5   PUNCTUATION WITH ITALICS

There are italic forms of most marks of punctuation. The type style (roman or italics) of the main part of any sentence will govern the style of the punctuation marks within or concluding it. If the main part of a sentence is in roman but an italic word within it immediately precedes a mark of punctuation, that mark will normally be in roman. However, if the punctuation mark occurs within a phrase or title which is entirely in italics, or if the punctuation mark belongs to the phrase in italics rather than to the sentence as a whole, the punctuation mark will be in italics:

> Where is a storm more brilliantly portrayed than in Conrad's *Typhoon?*
>
> In *Edmund Ironside; or, War Hath Made All Friends*, a play that survives in manuscript, we see this technique in operation.
>
> Kingsley followed this with *Westward Ho!*, perhaps his best-known novel.
>
> Who wrote *Who's Afraid of Virginia Woolf?*?

Do not follow the practice of substituting roman for italics in titles within italicized titles (e.g. *Understanding* Les Fleurs du mal*: Critical Readings*); in such cases, quotation marks should be used even if they do not figure in the original, e.g. *Understanding 'Les Fleurs du mal': Critical Readings*.

5.6   QUOTATION MARKS

See Chapter 9. For the use of quotation marks with the titles of poems, essays, etc., see 7.3.

5.7   ELLIPSES AND SQUARE BRACKETS

In quotations, points indicating an ellipsis (i.e. the omission of a portion of the text) should be enclosed within square brackets:

> Her enquiries [...] were not very favourably answered.

This practice makes it possible to distinguish between points indicating an ellipsis and points that occur in the original, as in the following quotation from Samuel Beckett:

> Will you never have done ... revolving it all?

The original punctuation is retained when it is possible to do so:

> When, in the course of human events, it becomes necessary for one people to dissolve the political bands which have connected them with another [...], a decent respect to the opinions of mankind requires that they should declare the causes which impel them to the separation.
>
> Outside the hut I stood bemused. [...] It was still morning and the smoke from the cookhouse rose straight to the leaden sky.

When the beginning of a sentence is omitted, the first word following the ellipsis can be capitalized even if it does not have a capital in the original:

> For the rest of the evening, von Igelfeld considered his response. [...] He could just ignore the article altogether.

(In the original, the passage abbreviated ends 'And finally, he could just ignore the article altogether'.)

One may also indicate a change of case in square brackets:

> Mrs Bennet felt that '[t]his was invitation enough'.

> '[A] young man of large fortune' had taken Netherfield.

See too 9.6 on omissions within quotations.

CAPITALS

6.1 GENERAL

Initial capitals should be used with restraint. In particular, adjectives deriving from nouns taking initial capitals are in many cases not capitalized (but see 6.3):

> Alps, alpine; Bible, biblical; Satan, satanic (but Satanic with reference to Satan himself)

Capitals must, however, be used for the initial letters of sentences and for the names of places, persons, nationalities, the days of the week, and months (but not for the seasons of the year). They are also to be used for the titles of laws, plans, wars, treaties, legal cases, and for specific institutions and other organizations (the Modern Humanities Research Association, the Poetry Book Club). Capitals are used also for unique events and periods (the Flood, the Iron Age, the Peasants' Revolt, the Reformation, the Enlightenment, the French Revolution, World War II, the Last Judgement) and for parts of books when referred to specifically (Chapter 9, Appendix A, Figure 8, Part 11). Names of the points of the compass are capitalized only when abbreviated (N.) or when they indicate a specific area (the North [of England], South America) or a political concept (the West). The corresponding adjectives are capitalized when they are part of an official name (Northern Ireland) or when they refer to political concepts rather than merely to geographical areas (Western Europe) but not otherwise (northern England). 'Middle' is capitalized in such fixed expressions as Middle East(ern), Middle Ages, Middle English.

Dictionaries are often inconsistent in their use or non-use of capitals for adjectives, verbs, and nouns deriving from names of peoples or languages. We recommend that capitals be used in such cases:

> Francophile, Gallicism, Italianist, Latinate

Note, however, that 'anglicize', 'anglophone', 'francophone', 'romanization', etc., are not capitalized, nor are 'arabic numerals' and 'roman type' (but 'the Arabic language', 'the Roman alphabet').

6.2   TITLES AND DIGNITIES

Capitals are used for titles and dignities when these appear in full or immediately preceding a personal name, or when they are used specifically, but not otherwise:

> The Archbishop of Canterbury and several other bishops were present, but Bishop Wilberforce was not.

When, after a first full reference, or with such reference understood, a title is used incompletely but still with specific application to an individual, the capital is retained:

> The Archbishop spoke first.

A word or phrase used as a substitute for, or an extension of, a personal name also takes initial capitals:

> the Iron Duke, Alfred the Great, the Dark Lady of the Sonnets

6.3   MOVEMENTS AND PERIODS

Capitals must be used for nouns and adjectives denoting cultural, philosophical, literary, critical, and artistic movements and periods when these are derived from proper nouns:

> Cartesian, Chomskyan, Christian, Erastian, Freudian, Platonism

They should also be used for literary and other movements when the use of a lower-case initial might cause confusion with the same word in a more general sense:

> a poet of the Romantic school
> a novel with a straightforwardly romantic plot

This covers the use of capitals when terms such as Conservative, Democrat(ic), Independent, Liberal, National(ist), Republican, Social(ist) refer to specific political parties or movements, e.g. the Independent Labour Party, the Social and Liberal Democrats, but not otherwise, e.g. 'a man of conservative (*or* liberal) views'.

For movements and periods with the prefix 'neo' and other compounds, see 6.5.

6.4   TITLES OF BOOKS AND OTHER WRITINGS

In most modern European languages except English and French, and in Latin and transliterated Slavonic languages, capitalization in the titles of books, series, articles, essays, poems, etc. follows the rules of capitalization in normal prose. That is, the first word and all proper nouns (in German all nouns) take an initial capital, and all other words take a lower-case initial:

> *La vida es sueño*; *El alcalde de Zalamea*; *Il seme sotto la neve*; *De senectute*; *Autorenlexikon der deutschen Gegenwartsliteratur*; Obras clássicas da literatura portuguesa

In English titles the initial letters of the first word and of all nouns, pronouns (except the relative 'that'), adjectives, verbs, adverbs, and subordinating conjunctions are capitalized, but those of articles, possessive determiners ('my', etc.), prepositions, and the co-ordinating conjunctions 'and', 'but', 'or', and 'nor' are not:

> (books) *Put Out More Flags*; *How Far Can You Go?*; *The Man Who Was Thursday*; *All's Well that Ends Well*; *Pride and Prejudice*; *A Voyage towards the South Pole*; (series) A Social History of the Welsh Language; (poems) *The Faerie Queene*; 'The Passionate Shepherd to his Love'

The first word of a subtitle following a colon is capitalized:

> *Strange Music: The Metre of the English Heroic Line*
> *The Wild Card of Reading: On Paul de Man*

but *or*, introducing an alternative title after a semi-colon, is not:

> *All for Love; or, The World Well Lost*

English works with foreign titles are normally capitalized according to the English convention rather than that of the language of the title:

> *Religio Medici*; 'Portrait d'une Femme'; 'La Figlia che Piange'

In French titles it is normally only the initial letters of the first word and of proper nouns that are capitalized. But if the first word is a definite article, the following noun and any preceding adjectives also take an initial capital:

> *Le Médecin malgré lui*; *Les Grands Cimetières sous la lune*; *Un début dans la vie*; *Une ténébreuse affaire*; *Du latin aux langues romanes*; *Nouveau cours de grammaire*; *Histoire de la littérature française*; *A la recherche du temps perdu*

However, for reasons of symmetry, capitals are sometimes used elsewhere:

> 'Le Corbeau et le Renard'; *Le Rouge et le Noir*

and titles consisting of a complete sentence do not take additional capitals:

> *Les dieux ont soif*; *La guerre de Troie n'aura pas lieu*

Capitalization in the titles of newspapers and journals is inconsistent. In particular, in Romance languages, initials of some or all nouns and adjectives are sometimes capitalized, e.g. *Le Bien Public, Il Corriere della Sera, Dernières Nouvelles d'Alsace, El País, La Repubblica, Revue de Linguistique Romane.* The safest procedure is to adopt the preferred style of each publication.

6.5 COMPOUNDS

Capitals should be retained after the prefix in hyphenated compound forms such as:

anti-Semitism, neo-Aristotelian, non-Christian, post-Darwinian, post-Impressionism, pre-Columbian

Both parts of the compound are capitalized in 'Pre-Raphaelite'.

The following unhyphenated forms, uncapitalized or capitalized as shown, are preferred:

neoclassical, neocolonial, neorealism, neoscholastic
Neoplatonism, Nonconformism, Presocratic

Archaeologists and historians, when referring to prehistoric eras, usually write them as one word, capitalized when a noun but not when an adjective:

before the Neolithic, neolithic sites

In titles and headings, all parts of the compound are normally capitalized:

Anglo-Jewish Studies, Non-Christian Communities, Seventeenth-Century Music, Post-Classical Literature

However, only the prefix is capitalized if both parts are essentially one word in hyphenated compounds formed with *re-*:

Democracy Re-established

6.6 ACCENTED CAPITALS

Accents should be retained on capitals in languages other than English, e.g.:

le Moyen-Âge, Éire, el Éufrates, Ólafsson

However, the French preposition *à* may drop the accent when capitalized (*A bientôt!* 'See you soon!').

6.7 SMALL CAPITALS

Small capitals are specially designed capitals, the height and visual weight of which approximate to those of lower-case letters. They are normally used for roman volume numbers, postal codes, professional and academic qualifications, 'AD', 'BC', 'CE', and 'BCE'. They also provide an alternative to italic and bold type in the typographic treatment of subheadings. For further guidance on roman numerals, see 8.3.

For the presentation of small capitals when preparing copy, see 1.3.3 and 1.3.15.

7 ITALICS

7.1 GENERAL

Avoid the use of italics for rhetorical emphasis. Any word or phrase individually discussed should, however, be in italics, and any interpretation of it in single quotation marks:

> He glosses *pale* as 'fenced land, park'.

It may also be desirable to use italics to distinguish one word or phrase from another, as, for example, in '23 April *not* 23ʳᵈ April'.

7.2 FOREIGN WORDS AND QUOTATIONS

Single words or short phrases in foreign languages not used as direct quotations should be in italics. Direct, acknowledged, or more substantial quotations should be in roman type (in small print or within single quotation marks). For the setting of quotations, see Chapter 9.

Foreign words and phrases which have passed into regular English usage should not be italicized, though the decision between italic and roman type may sometimes be a fine one. In doubtful instances it is usually best to use roman. The following are examples of words which are no longer italicized:

avant-garde	dilettante	milieu	role
cliché	ennui	par excellence	salon
debris	genre	per cent	status quo
denouement	leitmotif	résumé	vice versa

See also 2.2 and the *New Oxford Dictionary for Writers and Editors*.

Certain Latin words and abbreviations which are in common English usage are also no longer italicized. For example:

> cf., e.g., et al., etc., ibid., i.e., passim, viz.

Exceptions are made of the Latin *sic*, frequently used within quotations (see 5.3) and therefore conveniently differentiated by the use of italic, and of *circa* (abbreviated as *c.*, see 8.1). See also 11.3 on the use of such abbreviations.

7.3   TITLES OF BOOKS AND OTHER WRITINGS

Italics are used for the titles of all works individually published under their own titles: books, journals, plays, longer poems, pamphlets, and any other entire published works. However, titles such as 'the Bible', 'the Koran', and 'the Talmud' are printed in roman, as are titles of books of the Bible (see 11.2.8). Titles of series are not italicized, e.g. 'Theory and History of Literature'. The titles of chapters in books or of articles in books or journals should be in roman type enclosed within single quotation marks (see 11.2.3 and 11.2.4). The titles of poems, short stories, or essays which form part of a larger volume or other whole, or the first lines of poems used as titles, should also be given in roman type in single quotation marks:

> Théophile Gautier's 'L'Art'; Keats's 'Ode on a Grecian Urn'; Shelley's 'Music, When Soft Voices Die'; Joyce's 'The Dead'; Bacon's 'Of Superstition'

The titles of collections of manuscripts should be given in roman type without quotation marks (see 11.2.9). The titles of unpublished theses should be given in roman type in single quotation marks (see 11.2.6).

As recommended in 5.5, titles of other works which appear within an italicized title should be printed in italics and enclosed within single quotation marks:

> *An Approach to 'Hamlet'*

In the citation of legal cases the names of the contending parties are given in italics, but the intervening 'v.' (for 'versus') is in roman:

> *Bardell* v. *Pickwick*

7.4   TITLES OF FILMS, MUSICAL COMPOSITIONS, AND WORKS OF ART

Titles of films, substantial musical compositions, and works of art are italicized:

> *The Great Dictator*; *Il Trovatore*; *Elijah*; *Swan Lake*; Beethoven's *Eroica* Symphony; *Tapiola*; *Die schöne Müllerin*; *Goyescas*; *The Haywain*; *The Laughing Cavalier*; Epstein's *Christ in Majesty*

Descriptive or numerical titles such as the following, however, take neither italics (except in a reference to a publication or recording: see 11.2.11) nor quotation marks:

> Beethoven's Third Symphony; Bach's Mass in B minor; Mendelssohn's Andante and Scherzo; Piano Concerto no. 1 in B flat minor

Titles of songs and other short individual pieces (like those of poems; see 7.3) are given in roman and within single quotation marks:

'Who is Sylvia?'; 'La Marseillaise'; 'Mercury, the Winged Messenger' from Holst's *The Planets*

DATES, NUMBERS, CURRENCY, AND WEIGHTS & MEASURES

8.1 DATES

Dates should be given in the form '23 April 1564'. The name of the month should always appear in full between the day ('23' *not* '23ʳᵈ') and the year. No internal punctuation should be used except when a day of the week is mentioned, e.g. 'Friday, 12 October 2001'. If it is necessary to refer to a date in both Old and New Styles, the form '11/21 July 1605' should be used. For dates dependent upon the time of beginning the new year, the form '21 January 1564/5' should be used. When referring to a period of time, use the form 'from 1826 to 1850' (*not* 'from 1826–50'), 'from January to March 1970' (*not* 'from January–March 1970'). In citations of the era, 'BC', 'BCE', and 'CE' follow the year and 'AD' precedes it, and small capitals without full points are used:

> 54 BC, 54 BCE, 367 CE, AD 367

With reference to centuries, all of these, including 'AD', follow:

> in the third century AD

In references to decades, an *s* without an apostrophe should be used:

> the 1920s (*not* the 1920's)

In references to centuries the ordinal should be spelled out:

> the sixteenth century (*not* the 16th century)
> sixteenth-century drama

In giving approximate dates *circa* should be abbreviated as *c.* followed by a space:

> *c.* 1490, *c.* 300 BC

8.2 NUMBERS

Numbers up to and including one hundred, including ordinals, should be written in words when the context is not statistical. Figures should be used for volume, part, chapter, and page numbers; but note:

> The second chapter is longer than the first.

Figures are also used for years, including those below one hundred (see 8.1). However, numbers at the beginning of sentences and approximate numbers should be expressed in words, as should 'hundred', 'thousand', 'million', 'billion', etc., if they appear as whole numbers:

> Two hundred and forty-seven pages were written.
> The fire destroyed about five thousand books.
> She lived and wrote a thousand years ago.

Words should be preferred to figures where inelegance would otherwise result:

> He asked for ninety soldiers and received nine hundred and ninety.

In expressing inclusive numbers falling within the same hundred, the last two figures should be given, including any zero in the penultimate position:

> 13–15, 44–47, 100–22, 104–08, 1933–39

Where four-digit numbers do not fall within the same hundred, give both figures in full:

> 1098–1101

Dates of lifespans should be given in full, e.g. 1913–1991. Datespans before the Christian era should be stated in full since the shorter form could be misleading:

> The First Punic War (264–241 BC) (*not* 264–41 BC)

Numbers up to 9999 are written without a comma, e.g. 2589; those from 10,000 upwards take a comma, e.g. 125,397; those with seven or more digits take two or more commas, separating groups of three digits counting from the right, e.g. 9,999,000,000. However, where digits align in columns, in copy such as tables or accounts, commas must be consistently included or omitted in all numbers above 999.

8.3 ROMAN NUMERALS

The use of roman numerals should be confined to a few specific purposes:

(a) large capitals for the ordinals of monarchs, popes, etc. (Edward VII), and for major subdivisions within a text;

(b) small capitals for volume numbers of books (journals and series take arabic numerals), also for the acts of plays, for 'books' or other major subdivisions of long poems, novels, etc. (see 11.2.7), and for certain documents.

(c) small capitals for centuries in some languages other than English ('XVIᵉ siècle', 'siglo XVII'); however, in Cyrillic script large capitals are used;

(d) lower case for the preliminary pages of a book or journal (even if the original uses capitals), where these are numbered separately, and for minor subdivisions within a text; inclusive numbers are written out in full, e.g. 'xxiv–xxviii' not 'xxiv–viii'.

8.4   CURRENCY

Words should be used to express simple sums of money occurring in normal prose:

> The manuscript was sold for eight shillings in 1865.
> The reprint costs twenty-five pounds or forty euros.
> The fee was three hundred francs.

Names of foreign currencies should be given in their English form where one is in common use, e.g. 'mark' or 'deutschmark' (*not* 'deutsche Mark'), '[Swedish] crown', etc. Note too the use of English plurals such as 'drachmas', 'pfennigs' (*but* '[Italian] lire').

Sums of money which are awkward to express in words, or sums occurring in statistical tables, etc., may be written in figures. British currency before 1971 should be shown in the following form:

> The manuscript was sold for £197 12s. 6d. in 1965.

UK decimal currency should be expressed in pounds and pence separated by a full point on the line, not by a comma:

> £12.65 (not £12,65 or £12.65p)

Sums below one pound should be shown thus (without a full point after 'p'):

> 84p, 6p

The same conventions apply to sums expressed in euros, dollars, or yen:

> €250, $500, $8.95, 25c, ¥2000

Where it is necessary to specify that reference is to the American, Canadian, or some other dollar, an appropriate abbreviation precedes the symbol without a full point or a space:

> US$, C$ (*or* Can$), A$ (*or* Aus$), NZ$

In most cases, abbreviations for (Swiss) francs, Scandinavian crowns, or pre-2002 European currencies follow the figure, from which they are separated by a space, and are not followed by a full point, e.g. '95 F', '250 Kr' (BF, FF, SwF, DKr, NKr, SKr where it is necessary to specify Belgian, French,

Swiss, Danish, Norwegian, or Swedish currency). However, the abbreviation 'DM' for the German mark precedes the figure and is separated from it by a space, e.g. 'DM 8'.

The names of other currencies are best written out in full:

350 escudos, 500 pesetas, 20 roubles

8.5   WEIGHTS AND MEASURES

In non-statistical contexts express weights and measures in words:

He bought a phial of laudanum and an ounce of arsenic at a pharmacy two miles from Cheapside.

In statistical works or in subjects where frequent reference is made to them, weights and measures may be expressed in figures with appropriate abbreviations:

The priory is situated 3 km from the village of Emshall.
The same 13 mm capitals were used by three Madrid printers at different times.

Note that most such abbreviations do not take a full point or plural *s*:

1 kg, 15 kg, 1 mm, 6 cm, 15 m, 4 l (litres), 2 ft, 100 lb, 10 oz

but, to avoid ambiguity, use 'in.' for 'inch(es)'.

QUOTATIONS AND QUOTATION MARKS

9.1　GENERAL

Quotation marks should normally be reserved for indicating direct quotations, definitions of words, or for otherwise highlighting a word or phrase. Avoid the practice of using quotation marks as an oblique excuse for a loose, slang, or imprecise (and possibly inaccurate) word or phrase.

In quoted passages follow the original for spelling, capitalization, italics, and punctuation (but see 2.4, 5.3, 5.7, 9.3, and 9.4).

Prose quotations of no more than forty words in a single paragraph or verse quotations of no more than two lines are considered short quotations, and are to be treated as in 9.3 below. All other quotations should be treated as long quotations, as in 9.4 below. If, however, several short quotations come close together and are compared or contrasted or otherwise set out as examples, it may be appropriate to treat them together as a long quotation.

9.2　IN LANGUAGES OTHER THAN ENGLISH

Quotations in languages other than English are treated in the same way as those in English (see 7.2). Unless there are special reasons to the contrary, the forms of quotation marks in foreign languages («　»　„　"　etc.) should be normalized to English usage.

9.3　SHORT QUOTATIONS

Short quotations should be enclosed in single quotation marks and run on with the main text. If a verse quotation includes a line division, this should be marked with a spaced upright stroke (|).

> Balzac's famous observation, 'Je suis en train de devenir un génie', has generated much sceptical comment.

> 'I had seen birth and death | But had thought they were different', muses Eliot's Wise Man.

For a quotation within a quotation, double quotation marks should be used:

> Mrs Grose replies that 'Master Miles only said "We must do nothing but what she likes!" '.

If a short quotation is used at the end of a sentence, the final full point should be outside the closing quotation mark:

> Do not be afraid of what Stevenson calls 'a little judicious levity'.

This rule applies even when a quotation ends with a full point in the original, and when a quotation forms a complete sentence in the original but, as quoted, is integrated within a sentence of introduction or comment without intervening punctuation:

> We learn at once that 'Miss Brooke had that kind of beauty which seems to be thrown into relief by poor dress'.

For quotations which are either interrogatory or exclamatory, punctuation marks should appear both before and after the closing quotation mark:

> The pause is followed by Richard's demanding 'will no man say "Amen"?'.

> Why does Shakespeare give Malcolm the banal question 'Oh, by whom?'?

The final full point should precede the closing quotation mark only when the quotation forms a complete sentence and is separated from the preceding passage by a punctuation mark. Such a quotation may be interrupted:

> Wilde said, 'He found in stones the sermons he had already hidden there.'

> Soames added: 'Well, I hope you both enjoy yourselves.'

> Hardy's *Satires of Circumstance* was not well received. 'The gloom', wrote Lytton Strachey in his review of it, 'is not even relieved by a little elegance of diction.'

In this last example, the comma after 'gloom' follows the quotation mark as there is no comma in the original. Contrast:

> 'It is a far, far better thing that I do,' Carton asserts, 'than I have ever done.'

Here the original has a comma after 'I do'. But when the quotation ends in a question mark or an exclamation mark, it is not followed by a comma:

> 'What think you of books?' said he.

When a short quotation is followed by a reference in parentheses, the final punctuation should follow the closing parenthesis:

> He assumes the effect to be 'quite deliberate' (p. 29).

> There is no reason to doubt the effect of this 'secret humiliation' (Book 6, Chapter 52).

9.4 LONG QUOTATIONS

Long quotations should be broken off by an increased space from the preceding and following lines of typescript. A long quotation should never be used in the middle of a sentence of the main text: it is unreasonable to expect the reader to carry the sense of a sentence across a quotation several lines in length.

Long quotations should not be enclosed within quotation marks. A quotation occurring within such a long quotation should be in single quotation marks; if a further quotation occurs within that, double quotation marks should be used. Foreign forms of quotation marks (see 9.2) should not be preserved unless there are special reasons for doing so.

Prose quotations, including the first line, should not be indented; verse quotations should follow the lineation and indentation of the original. These longer quotations should be double spaced and they should be marked by a vertical line in the margin to indicate that they are to be printed in the form which is standard for the publication concerned. To assist the typesetter, a long quotation should be marked with an encircled note 'verse' or 'prose' in the margin if there is any possibility of doubt. When printed, a long quotation may be distinguished from the main text by setting it in a smaller size, indenting it, or a combination of the two. The preparation and marking of the typescript in the manner described would, however, be suitable for any likely style of printing.

Long quotations should normally end with a full point; even though the original may use other punctuation, there is no need (except for a question mark or exclamation mark) to preserve this at the end of a quotation.

Avoid interpolations indicating source that introduce square brackets into the opening lines of long quotations, e.g.:

> This play [writes Dr Johnson, referring to *Cymbeline*] has many just sentiments, some natural dialogues, and some pleasing scenes, but they are obtained at the expense of much incongruity.

The need for any such formulation can be eliminated by some such rephrasing as the following:

> Referring to *Cymbeline*, Dr Johnson writes:
>
> > This play has many just sentiments, some natural dialogues, and some pleasing scenes.

A reference in parentheses after a long quotation should always be placed outside the closing full point, and without a full point of its own (see the first example in 9.5).

9.5   QUOTATIONS FROM PLAYS

Where a quotation from a play is longer than about forty words, or two lines of verse, it should be treated as a long quotation (see 9.4). Whilst the spelling and punctuation within the text should be preserved, general rules may be applied to the treatment of speakers' names and stage directions.

Where a single quotation contains both prose and blank verse, special care should be taken to indicate the point at which one ends and the other begins. Where a line of text is indented in the original, it should be typed as near as possible to its original position and the typesetter instructed in an encircled marginal note to 'follow typescript for indent'.

Most academic publishers have well-established conventions that should be observed when preparing a typescript. The following rules apply to MHRA publications in which quotations from plays appear.

Prose quotations are set full out with the speakers' names in small capitals, without final punctuation but followed by a space. Second and subsequent lines of a speech are indented. Stage directions within a line of text are set in italic type within roman parentheses. If a stage direction immediately follows a speaker's name, the space preceding the text is placed at the end of the stage direction, after the closing parenthesis. Stage directions which occupy a line on their own are indented further than the text, and set in italic type without parentheses. No extra space is inserted between speakers. Thus for example:

BRASSBOUND   It will teach other scoundrels to respect widows and orphans. Do
   you forget that there is such a thing as justice?
LADY CICELY (*gaily shaking out the finished coat*)   Oh, if you are going to dress
   yourself in ermine and call yourself Justice, I give you up. You are just your
   uncle over again; only he gets £5000 a year for it, and you do it for nothing.
      She holds the coat up to see whether any further repairs are needed.
BRASSBOUND (*sulkily*)   You twist my words very cleverly. (*Captain Brassbound's
   Conversion*, II)

In verse quotations, the speakers' names are positioned to the left of the text:

MACBETH   Prithee, peace!
                 I dare do all that may become a man;
                 Who dares do more, is none.
LADY MACBETH   What beast was't then
                 That made you break this enterprise to me?
                 When you durst do it, then you were a man;
                 And to be more than what you were, you would
                 Be so much more the man.

9.6 OMISSIONS

Omissions within prose quotations should be marked by an ellipsis (three points within square brackets; see 5.7). Omitted lines of verse should be marked by an ellipsis on a separate line:

> I am not covetous for gold,
> [...]
> But if it be a sin to covet honour
> I am the most offending soul alive.

It is not normally necessary to use an ellipsis at the beginning or end of a quotation; almost all quotations will be taken from a larger context and there is usually no need to indicate this obvious fact unless the sense of the passage quoted is manifestly incomplete.

9.7 COPYRIGHT AND PERMISSIONS

It is the responsibility of an author to obtain any necessary permission for quotation of copyright material. The author should ensure that permission to reproduce material in all territories and all media (e.g. print and electronic) is granted.

Normally it is unnecessary to seek permission for the quotation of brief passages in a scholarly work, but it is not possible to give a definitive ruling to indicate when it is necessary to seek permission: copyright laws are not the same in all countries, and publishers hold differing views on the subject. If in doubt, authors should consult their editors.

In general it may be said that the length of the quoted passage and the use to which it is put should be fair to the author and publisher of the work quoted in that nothing is done to diminish the value of their publication.

Complete items such as tables, illustrations, and poems must not be reproduced without permission. (See also 1.3.12.)

FOOTNOTES AND ENDNOTES

10.1 GENERAL

The term 'notes' as used in this chapter applies equally to footnotes and to endnotes (i.e. references printed at the end of an article, chapter, or book).

Notes are an interruption to the reader and should be kept down to what is strictly necessary. They are intended primarily for documentation and for the citation of sources relevant to the text. They should not be used to provide additional bibliographical material on the general subject being treated, but which is not directly needed. Nor should they normally include extra expository material. Such material, if apposite and useful, is often better incorporated into the text or added as an appendix. Only after the most careful consideration should it be included in a note.

All notes, whether or not they form complete sentences, should end with full points.

10.2 METHODS OF LIMITING NOTES

Simple references (such as line numbers or page references to a book already cited in full) can usually be incorporated in the text, normally in parentheses after quotations. A string of note references to the same text can be avoided by stating after the first full note citation: 'Further references [to this edition, etc.] are given after quotations in the text.' (See also 11.3.)

The number of notes can often be kept down by grouping together, in one note, references to several sources mentioned close together in the same paragraph. In particular, adjacent references to several pages of the same publication should be cited together in a single note. No note, however, should document references for more than one paragraph.

Notes should not repeat information already clear from the text: if, for example, the author has been named before a quotation there is no need to repeat the name in a note reference. If there is a bibliography to a book or article, notes can also be reduced.

10.3 POSITION AND NUMBERING

Wherever possible, a note reference number should be placed at the end of a sentence. Notes should be marked in the typescript by superior (superscript) numbers, with no punctuation (full points, parentheses, etc.), in sequence throughout an article or chapter. A note reference number should follow any punctuation except a dash, which it should precede. It should appear at the end of a quotation, not following the author's name if that precedes the quotation.

A note reference number in the text should never be repeated to refer to the same note; if the same material has to be referred to again, a parenthetical reference in the text — '(see note 1 above)' — is the best method, though a new note using those words is a possible alternative.

Do not attach a note number to a heading or subheading; an asterisk may, however, be used to indicate a general note to an entire chapter. Nor should a note number (or, indeed, an asterisk) be attached to the title of an article; a note attached to the first or last sentence, or an unnumbered note preceding the numbered ones, is preferable.

REFERENCES

11.1   GENERAL

References (in the body of the text or in notes) should document the information offered, to allow the reader to check the source of a quotation or the evidence on which an argument is based. A reference must therefore enable the reader to find the source referred to as quickly and easily as possible.

A work of literature should be quoted or referred to in a satisfactory scholarly edition. If a literary or critical work is published both in Britain and overseas, the British edition should be used unless there are special reasons for doing otherwise. If an edition other than the first is used, this should be stated. If an unrevised reprint is used (such as a modern facsimile reprint of an out-of-print work or a paperback reissue of an earlier book), the publication details of the original edition as well as of the reprint should be given. Details of original publication should also be provided where an article from a journal is reprinted in an anthology of criticism (see 11.2.3): a reader looking for the article in a library is often more likely to find the original journal than the anthology. In referring to works of literature of which several editions may be available, it is often helpful to give the reader more information than merely the page number of the edition used:

> p. 235 (Book III, Chapter 4)

Similarly, when quoting a letter from a collection, it may be helpful to cite the date as well as the page number:

> p. 281 (23 April 1864)

Full references to well-known works (*OED*, *DNB*, etc.) are normally unnecessary, though for encyclopedias and biographical dictionaries of multiple authorship it is often relevant to name the writer of the article cited.

11.2   FORMS OF REFERENCE

11.2.1 GENERAL

Except when the author-date system (see 11.4) is used or when full details are given in a separate bibliography, the first reference to a book, article, or other publication should be given in full and later references in an easily identifiable abbreviated form (see 11.3).

11.2.2 BOOKS

Full references should be given as in the following examples of monographs, edited volumes, and editions of texts:

(i)   Tom McArthur, *Worlds of Reference: Lexicography, Learning and Language from the Clay Tablet to the Computer* (Cambridge: Cambridge University Press, 1986), p. 59.

(ii)   Jean Starobinski, *Montaigne in Motion*, trans. by Arthur Goldhammer (Chicago: University of Chicago Press, 1986), p. 174.

(iii) H. Munro Chadwick and N. Kershaw Chadwick, *The Growth of Literature*, 3 vols (Cambridge: Cambridge University Press, 1932–40; repr. 1986), I, p. xiii.

(iv)   José Amador de los Ríos, *Historia crítica de la literatura española*, 7 vols (Madrid: the author, 1861–65; repr. Madrid: Gredos, 1969), VI (1865), 44–54.

(v)   Debra Linowitz Wentz, *Fait et fiction: les formules pédagogiques des 'Contes d'une grand-mère' de George Sand* (Paris: Nizet, 1985), p. 9.

(vi)   *Approaches to Teaching Voltaire's 'Candide'*, ed. by R. Waldinger (New York: Modern Language Association of America, 1987), p. 3.

(vii) *Dictionary of the Middle Ages*, ed. by Joseph R. Strayer and others, 13 vols (New York: Scribner, 1982–89), VI (1985), 26.

(viii) Carlos Fuentes, *Aura*, ed. by Peter Standish, Durham Modern Language Series: Hispanic Texts, 1 (Durham: University of Durham, 1986), pp. 12–16 (p. 14).

(ix)   *Emily Dickinson: Selected Letters*, ed. by Thomas H. Johnson, 2nd edn (Cambridge, MA: Harvard University Press, 1985), pp. 194–97.

(x)   *Boswell: The English Experiment 1785–1789*, ed. by Irma S. Lustig and Frederick A. Pottle, The Yale Edition of the Private Papers of James Boswell (London: Heinemann; New York: McGraw Hill, 1986), pp. 333–37.

(xi)   *The Works of Thomas Nashe*, ed. by Ronald B. McKerrow, 2nd edn, rev. by F. P. Wilson, 5 vols (Oxford: Blackwell, 1958), III, 94–98 (pp. 95–96).

(xii) Hugo von Hofmannsthal, *Sämtliche Werke*, ed. by Rudolf Hirsch and others (Frankfurt a.M.: Fischer, 1975–), XIII: *Dramen*, ed. by Roland Haltmeier (1986), pp. 12–22.

(xiii) Sophocles, *Fabulae*, ed. by H. Lloyd-Jones and N. G. Wilson (Oxford: Clarendon Press, 1990), pp. 59-118.

(xiv) Cornelius Tacitus, *Opera minora*, ed. by M. Winterbottom and R. M. Ogilvie (Oxford: Clarendon Press, 1975), pp. v-x.

The information should be given in the following order:

1. *Author*: The author's name should normally be given as it appears on the title page; forenames should precede surnames and should not be reduced to initials. However, classical names should be given in the nominative form even if the genitive is used on the title page: see examples (xiii) and (xiv). The names of up to three authors should be given in full; for works by more than three authors the name of only the first should be given, followed by 'and others' (see example (vii)). If the author's name is more conveniently included within the title (as, for example, in editions of 'Works'), or if the book is an edited collection or anthology, the title will appear first (see examples (vi), (vii), (ix)–(xi)).

2. *Title*: The title should be given as it appears on the title page (although very long titles may be suitably abbreviated) and italicized. A colon should always be used to separate title and subtitle, even where the punctuation on the title page is different or (as often happens) non-existent. For books in English, capitalize the initial letter of the first word after the colon and of all principal words throughout the title (see examples (i) and (x)); for titles in other languages, follow the capitalization rules for the language in question (see 6.4 and examples (iv), (v), (xii), (xiv)). If figures occur in titles, these should also be italicized (see example (x)). Titles of other works occurring within the title should be enclosed in quotation marks (see examples (v) and (vi)). For books (usually older works) with alternative titles, punctuation before and after 'or' should be as follows:

   > *The Queen; or, The Excellency of her Sex*
   > *All for Love; or, The World Well Lost*

3. *Editor, Translator, etc.*: The names of editors, etc. should be treated in the same way as those of authors (as set out above) with regard to forenames and number to be given; they should be preceded by the accepted abbreviated forms 'ed. by', 'trans. by', 'rev. by' (see examples (ii) and (vi)–(xiv)). For multi-volume works where there is more than one editor or group of editors involved, the information should be conveyed as in examples (vii), (x), and (xii); but see example (xi) where only one editor is involved.

4. *Series*: If a book is part of a numbered series, the series title and the number (in arabic numerals) should be given (see example (viii)). However, the name of the series may be omitted if it is unnumbered,

unless the series title itself conveys important information (see example (x)). Series titles should not be italicized or put between quotation marks.

5.   *Edition*: If the edition used is other than the first, this should be stated in the form '2nd edn', '5th edn', 'rev. edn' (see examples (ix) and (xi)).

6.   *Number of Volumes*: If the work is in more than one volume, the number of volumes should be given in the form '2 vols' (see examples (iii), (iv), (vii), (xi)). Foreign equivalents, such as 'tome', 'Band', 'tomo', should usually be rendered as 'vol.'.

7.   *Details of Publication*: The place of publication, the name of the publisher, and the date of publication should be enclosed in parentheses; a colon separates the place from the publisher, a comma separates the publisher from the date. Any detail of publication which is not given in the book itself but can be ascertained should be enclosed in square brackets, e.g. '[Paris]', '[1987]'. For details that are assumed but uncertain, use the form '[Paris(?)]', '[1987(?)]'. If any detail is unknown and cannot be ascertained, the following abbreviated forms of reference should be used: '[n.p.]' (= no place), '[n. pub.]' (= no publisher), '[n.d.]' (= no date). Do not use square brackets in a reference for any other purpose (for example, when the reference is already in parentheses), otherwise the impression may be conveyed that the information in square brackets is uncertain.

In giving the place of publication, the current English forms of place-names should be used where these exist (e.g. Geneva, Milan, Munich, Vienna; see 3.1.1). The two-letter abbreviated forms of names of American states (see 4.5) should be included if there is danger of confusion (e.g. Cambridge, MA; Athens, GA). These are not required if the name of the state appears in the name of the publisher (e.g. Athens: University of Georgia Press). For books published by the same publisher in more than one place, it is normally sufficient to refer only to the first. Place of publication should be omitted only when (as, for example, in a bibliographical article) there are likely to be a great many references to books published at one place. In these circumstances, provide an early note in the form of 'Place of publication of all books cited is London [or Paris, etc.] unless otherwise stated'.

The name of the publishing house (preceded by a colon) should be given without secondary matter such as an initial definite article, '& Co.', 'Ltd', or 'S.A.'. 'Press', 'Verlag', 'Editorial', etc. are usually omitted where the name of the house is that of its proprietor or founder.

Thus for example:

Éditions de la Femme, Harvester Press, Oxford University Press, Clarendon Press, Blackwell, Mellen, Laterza

It is not normally necessary to include forenames or initials of publishers, unless there are two or more with the same surname:

Brewer (*not* D. S. Brewer); Heinemann (*not* William Heinemann)

Where a publisher's name includes 'and' or '&', the conjunction should be given in the form which appears on the title page:

Thames and Hudson; Grant & Cutler

A book which has more than one place of publication and a different publisher in each place should be referred to as in example (x).

Details of facsimile reprints of old books should be given as in example (iii) where the original publisher is responsible for the reprint, and as in example (iv) where different publishers are involved. Example (iv) also illustrates the appropriate form of reference to a work published by its author.

A reference to a work in several volumes published over a period of years but now complete should state the number of volumes and give inclusive dates of publication and the date of the volume specifically referred to where this is not the first or last in the series (see examples (iii), (iv), (vii)). But if a work in several volumes is incomplete and still in the process of publication, the date of the first volume should be stated followed by a dash, and the date of the individual volume being cited should be added in parentheses after the volume number (see example (xii)). In some instances (for example, if each volume of a set has a different editor) it may be more appropriate to give publication details only for the volume cited.

8. *Volume Number*: In a multi-volume work the number of the volume referred to should be given in small capital roman numerals, followed where necessary by the year of publication in parentheses (see examples (iv), (vii), (xii)). It is very rarely necessary to insert 'vol.' before the volume number.

9. *Page Numbers*: If a volume number is not cited or if it is distant (as in example (xii)), 'p.' or 'pp.' should be inserted before the page number(s). It is customary to omit 'p./pp.' when the volume number immediately or closely precedes (see examples (iv), (vii), (xi)), unless the page number(s) are also in roman numerals (see example (iii)). If an entry relates to

several successive pages, the first and last page numbers of the span should always be stated:

> pp. 201–09 (*not* pp. 201 ff.)

If it is necessary to indicate a particular reference within a page span, the specific page number(s) should be given in parentheses (see examples (viii), (xi)).

Note that 'folio', 'recto', and 'verso' are abbreviated thus:

> fol. 3^r, fol. 127^v, fols 17^v–22^r

11.2.3 CHAPTERS OR ARTICLES IN BOOKS

Full references should be given as in the following examples:

(i) Martin Elsky, 'Words, Things, and Names: Jonson's Poetry and Philosophical Grammar', in *Classic and Cavalier: Essays on Jonson and the Sons of Ben*, ed. by Claude J. Summers and Ted-Larry Pebworth (Pittsburgh: University of Pittsburgh Press, 1982), pp. 31–55 (p. 41).

(ii) Fanni Bogdanow, 'The *Suite du Merlin* and the Post-Vulgate *Roman du Graal*', in *Arthurian Literature in the Middle Ages: A Collaborative History*, ed. by Roger Sherman Loomis (Oxford: Clarendon Press, 1959), pp. 325–35.

(iii) R. P. Calcraft, 'The Lover as Icarus: Góngora's "Qué de invidiosos montes levantados"', in *What's Past Is Prologue: A Collection of Essays in Honour of L. J. Woodward*, ed. by Salvador Bacarisse and others (Edinburgh: Scottish Academic Press, 1984), pp. 10–16 (p. 12).

(iv) Luis T. González-del-Valle, 'Lo interpersonal en *Presentimiento de lobos*: un estudio de los modos de transmisión', in *Estudios en honor de Ricardo Gullón*, ed. by Luis T. González-del-Valle and Darío Villanueva (Lincoln, NE: Society of Spanish and Spanish-American Studies, 1984), pp. 141–53.

When a second item from a volume previously mentioned is to be listed, use an abbreviated form, as in this example referring to the volume in (ii) above:

(v) Eugène Vinaver, 'The Prose *Tristan*', in *Arthurian Literature*, ed. by Loomis, pp. 339–47.

Similar conventions apply in the case of an article in an issue of a journal that has its own editor and a title:

(vi) E. Glyn Lewis, 'Attitudes to the Planned Development of Welsh', in *The Sociology of Welsh*, ed. by Glyn Williams (= *International Journal of the Sociology of Language*, 66 (1987)), pp. 11–26.

The information should be given in the following order:

Author's name, exactly as it appears in the book (see 11.2.2, *Author*)

Title of chapter or article in single quotation marks

The word 'in' (preceded by a comma) followed by title, editor's name, and full publication details of book as in 11.2.2

First and last page numbers of item cited, preceded by 'pp.'

Page number(s), in parentheses and preceded by 'p.' or 'pp.', of the particular reference (if necessary)

A colon should be used to separate title and subtitle. For titles in English, capitalize the initial letter of the first word after the colon and all principal words throughout the title (including the subtitle) (see examples (i), (iii), (vi)); for titles in other languages, follow the capitalization rules for the language in question (see 6.4 and example (iv)). The titles of works of literature occurring within the titles of chapters or articles should be italicized or placed within quotation marks, whichever is appropriate (see examples (ii), (iii), (iv)). If quotation marks are used within the title, they should be double (see example (iii)), since single quotation marks will already have been used to enclose the title itself (see 9.3).

If a particular page within a chapter or article is to be indicated, the full page span should nevertheless be given in the first full citation and a reference to the particular page added in parentheses (see examples (i) and (iii)).

Reference to an article in a book which has previously been published in a journal should take one of the following forms:

Alfred L. Kellogg and Louis A. Haselmayer, 'Chaucer's Satire of the Pardoner', *PMLA*, 66 (1951), 251–77 (repr. in Alfred L. Kellogg, *Chaucer, Langland, Arthur: Essays in Middle English Literature* (New Brunswick, NJ: Rutgers University Press, 1972), pp. 212–44).

Edwin Honig, 'Calderón's Strange Mercy Play', in *Critical Essays on the Theatre of Calderón*, ed. by Bruce W. Wardropper (New York: New York University Press, 1965), pp. 167–92 (first publ. in *Massachusetts Review*, 3 (1961), 80–107).

The second form should be used if the collection of essays is more generally available than the individual journal (which may be old or obscure) or if reference is going to be made to several articles in the collection, thus facilitating the use of a short form for later references (see 11.3).

Other subdivisions in books, when separately cited, should be treated as seems appropriate according to this general pattern. Thus:

Troilus and Criseyde, in *The Works of Geoffrey Chaucer*, ed. by F. N. Robinson, 2nd edn (London: Oxford University Press, 1957), pp. 385–479.

Marqués de Santillana, *Infierno de los enamorados*, in *Poesías completas*, ed. by Miguel Ángel Pérez Priego, I, Clásicos Alhambra, 25 (Madrid: Alhambra, 1983), pp. 225–58.

II.2.4 ARTICLES IN JOURNALS

The first reference should be given in full in a form similar to that in the following examples:

(i) Richard Hillyer, 'In More than Name Only: Jonson's "To Sir Horace Vere"', *MLR*, 85 (1990), 1–11 (p. 8).

(ii) L. T. Topsfield, '*Jois, Amors* and *Fin' Amors* in the Poetry of Jaufre Rudel', *Neuphilologische Mitteilungen*, 71 (1970), 277–305 (p. 279).

(iii) Victor Skretkowicz, 'Devices and their Narrative Function in Sidney's *Arcadia*', *Emblematica*, 1 (1986), 267–92.

(iv) J. D. Spikes, 'The Jacobean History Play and the Myth of the Elect Nation', *Renaissance Drama*, n.s., 8 (1970), 117–49.

(v) Robert F. Cook, '*Baudouin de Sebourc*: un poème édifiant?', *Olifant,* 14 (1989), 115–35 (pp. 118–19).

(vi) Eduardo Urbina, 'Don Quijote, *puer–senex*: un tópico y su transformación paródica en el *Quijote*', *Journal of Hispanic Philology*, 12 (1987–88), 127–38.

(vii) James Trainer, 'Sophie an Ludwig Tieck: neu identifizierte Briefe', *Jahrbuch der deutschen Schillergesellschaft*, 24 (1980), 162–81 (p. 179).

(viii) Maurizio Perugi, 'James Sully e la formazione dell'estetica pascoliana', *Studi di filologia italiana*, 42 (1984), 225–309.

(ix) Nathalie Z. Davis, 'Beyond the Market: Books as Gifts in Sixteenth-Century France', *Transactions of the Royal Historical Society*, 5th ser., 33 (1983), 69–88.

The information should be given in the following order:

Author's name, exactly as it appears in the article (see II.2.2, *Author*)

Title of article, in single quotation marks

Title of journal, italicized

Series number, in arabic numerals

Volume number, in arabic numerals

Year(s) of publication, in parentheses unless there is no volume number

First and last page numbers of article cited, not preceded by 'pp.'

Page number(s), in parentheses and preceded by 'p.' or 'pp.', of the particular reference (if necessary)

The use of the colon to separate the title and subtitle in an article, the norms for capitalization within the title and subtitle, the treatment of the titles of works of literature occurring within the titles of articles, and references to particular pages within an article are, as the examples illustrate, treated in the same way as for articles in books (see 11.2.3). Note, however, that the page span of articles in journals is not preceded by 'pp.'.

Only the main title of a journal should be given. Any subtitle and the place of publication should be omitted unless they serve to distinguish between two journals of the same name. An initial definite or indefinite article should be omitted except when the title consists of the article and one other word, e.g. *La Linguistique*. If the journal title is abbreviated to initials, full points should not be used (see example (i) and 4.4). The titles of journals should be abbreviated only when the abbreviation is likely to be familiar to all readers (e.g. *PMLA*), otherwise the title should be given in full. If there are to be several references to the same journal, an abbreviated title should be indicated after the first full reference (e.g. *French Studies* (hereafter *FS*)) or in a preliminary list of abbreviations. For the proceedings of learned societies, etc., the name of the organization should be italicized as part of the title (e.g. *Proceedings of the British Academy*).

The volume number should be given in arabic numerals, no matter what the style preferred by the journal (e.g. *Medium Ævum*, 58, *not* LVIII). The number should not be preceded by 'vol.'. If a journal has restarted publication with a new numbering, this should be indicated by e.g. 'n.s.' (= 'new series') or '5th ser.' before the volume number (see examples (iv) and (ix)).

If the separate issues of a journal cover an academic year rather than a calendar year, this should be indicated as in example (vi). If the publication of a volume of a journal has been considerably delayed, the actual year of publication should be given in square brackets after the official year (e.g. 1983 [1987]).

Normally it will not be necessary to cite the month or season of publication or the part number of an issue of a journal, unless the part numbers are individually paginated, in which case the information should be given:

Lionel Trilling, 'In Mansfield Park', *Encounter*, 3.3 (September 1954), 9–19.

José Luis Pardo, 'Filosofía y clausura de la modernidad', *Revista de Occidente*, 66 (November 1986), 35–47.

E. Iukina, 'Dostoinstvo cheloveka', *Novyi mir*, 1984.12, 245–48.

For the formulation to be used in referring to a journal article in an issue that has its own editor and a title, see 11.2.3, example (vi).

II.2.5   Articles in Newspapers and Magazines

References to articles in newspapers or magazines require only the date of issue (day, month, and year), the section where relevant (e.g. 'Reviews section', 'section G2'), and the page number(s) (but note that these may vary between editions); volume or part numbers should not be included:

> Michael Schmidt, 'Tragedy of Three Star-Crossed Lovers', *Daily Telegraph*, 1 February 1990, p. 14.
>
> Jonathan Friedland, 'Across the Divide', *Guardian*, 15 January 2002, section G2, pp. 10–11.
>
> Jacques-Pierre Amette, 'Thé et désespoir', *Le Point*, 8 October 1989, p. 18.
>
> Carlos Bousoño, 'La ebriedad de un poeta puro', *El País*, 21 May 1989, p. 17.

Initial '*The*' or '*A*' is normally omitted when citing English-language newspapers and magazines, with the exception of *The Times*. The date of issue (with the month always in English) should be given between commas, not parentheses, and the page number(s) should be preceded by 'p.' or 'pp.'. Otherwise the method of citation is the same as for other articles (see 11.2.3 and 11.2.4).

II.2.6   Theses and Dissertations

The titles of unpublished theses and dissertations should be in roman type within single quotation marks; capitalization should follow the conventions of the language in question (see 6.4). The degree level (where known), university, and date should be in parentheses:

> R. J. Ingram, 'Historical Drama in Great Britain from 1935 to the Present' (unpublished doctoral thesis, University of London, Birkbeck College, 1988), p. 17.
>
> Diedrich Diederischen, 'Shakespeare und das deutsche Märchendrama' (unpublished doctoral thesis, University of Hamburg, 1952), p. 91.
>
> Mary Taylor, 'The Legend of Apollonius of Tyre in Spanish and French Literature before 1500' (unpublished master's thesis, University of Manchester, 1977), pp. 45–47.
>
> James-Louis Boyle, 'Marcel Proust et les écrivains anglais' (unpublished thesis, University of Paris, 1953), p. 22.

Note that American universities distinguish between a master's 'thesis' and a doctoral 'dissertation':

> Barbara Jean Trisler, 'A Comparative Study of the Character Portrayal of Celestina and Other Golden Age Celestinesque Protagonists' (unpublished master's thesis, University of Oklahoma, 1977), p. 4.

William Eugene Simeone, 'Sir Richard Fanshawe: An Account of his Life and Writings' (unpublished doctoral dissertation, University of Pennsylvania, 1950), pp. 166–79.

If a published abstract of an unpublished thesis or dissertation is known to exist, the information should be given:

Jon Vaden Anderson, 'A Woman's Work: Feminist Tensions in the Victorian Novel' (unpublished doctoral dissertation, Texas Christian Univ., 1997; abstract in *Dissertation Abstracts International*, 58 (1997), 880A).

11.2.7 PLAYS AND LONG WORKS

The first full reference to a play or long work should indicate the edition used (see 11.2.2 (xi) and (xii)). Small capital roman numerals should be used for the numbers of acts of plays, and for the numbers of 'books' and other major subdivisions. Smaller subdivisions (scenes, cantos, chapters, etc.) and line numbers are usually indicated by arabic numerals. Later references and the identification of quotations should be given in the form: *Macbeth*, III. 4. 99–107, *Samson Agonistes*, I. 819. Note that figures in references should be separated by full points (not commas) and spaces, e.g.

The Merchant of Venice, II. 3. 10; *The Faerie Queene*, III. 8. 26; *Paradise Lost*, IX. 342–50; *Aeneid*, VI. 215–18; *Inferno*, III. 9; *City of God*, XIX. 2

11.2.8 THE BIBLE

References should be in the following form: Isaiah 22. 17; II Corinthians 5. 13–15. Note that books of the Bible are not italicized; roman numerals are used for the numbers of books, arabic numerals (separated by a full point) for chapters and verses.

11.2.9 MANUSCRIPTS

Names of repositories and collections should be given in full in the first instance and an abbreviated form should be used for subsequent references. The degree of abbreviation which may be acceptable will depend upon the frequency with which a particular repository, collection, or manuscript is referred to and upon any possible ambiguities. The names of manuscript collections should be given in roman type without quotation marks and the citation of manuscripts within collections should be according to the system of classification of the repository.

The following examples show a suggested method of citation for first references and possible models for later references. Note that, because of the danger of ambiguity, the abbreviations 'fol.' and 'fols' are preferred to 'f.' and 'ff.'. The abbreviated and superscript forms for 'recto' and 'verso' are also preferred.

First reference:	London, British Library, MS Cotton Caligula D III, fol. 15
Later references:	MS Cotton Caligula D III, fols 17^v–19^r
First reference:	Oxford, Bodleian Library, MS Bodley 277
Later references:	MS Bodley 277
First reference:	Sheffield Central Library, MS Fitzwilliam E.209
Later references:	Sheffield CL, MS Fitzwilliam E.209
First reference:	Paris, Bibliothèque nationale (BN), MS fonds français 1124
Later references:	BN, MS f. fr. 1124
First reference:	Florence, Biblioteca Riccardiana (BRF), MS 2306
Later references:	BRF, MS 2306, fol. 10^r
First reference:	Paris, Archives Nationales (AN), H.486 bis. 172
Later references:	AN, H.486 bis. 172

11.2.10   ONLINE PUBLICATIONS

11.2.10.1   GENERAL

Recent years have seen a rapid growth in publishing on the Internet (and on the World Wide Web in particular), and it has become more and more common to cite material published through this medium. Authors should exercise the same discretion in considering the quality and value of material published on the Internet as they would for material published by more traditional means.

It is not uncommon for Internet resources to change location on the server to which they were originally published, and even for them to be moved to a different server. Internet publications will often prove harder to pin down than their print equivalents, but systems such as DOI (Digital Object Identifier) that provide persistent identifiers for information resources are now used widely. (See also 11.2.10.2.)

As far as possible, follow the style used for printed publications as detailed above. Information should be given in the following order:

Author's name

Title of item

Title of complete work/resource

Publication details (volume, issue, date)

Full address (Universal Resource Locator (URL)) or DOI of the resource (in angle brackets)

Date at which the resource was consulted (in square brackets)

Location of passage cited (in parentheses)

11.2.10.2 ONLINE ARTICLES

The following is an example of how to refer to an article published in a Web-based journal:

> Steve Sohmer, 'The Lunar Calendar of Shakespeare's *King Lear*', *Early Modern Literary Studies*, 5.2 (1999) <http://purl.oclc.org/emls/05-2/sohmlear.htm> [accessed 28 January 2000] (para. 3 of 17)

Take care to follow the format of the URL exactly and remember that addresses are case-sensitive. URLs should be cited in full, including the indication of the relevant protocol (http, https, ftp, etc.). Ideally the address should not be divided over two lines, but if this cannot be avoided, break at a forward slash and do not introduce a hyphen.

Give the date on which the relevant section of the resource was last accessed; this will ensure that the accuracy of your reference will not be undermined by any subsequent changes to the resource. Where page numbers or numbered paragraphs appear in the original document, they can be used to give the location of a citation. Do not attempt to infer page or line numbers from on-screen documents since they may vary according to the browser used.

Articles published online that have a DOI should be cited thus:

> Els Jongeneel, 'Art and Divine Order in the *Divina Commedia*', *Literature and Theology*, 21 (2007) <doi: 10.1093/litthe/frm008>

11.2.10.3 ONLINE DATABASES

Online databases may be unique electronic publications, or they may provide collections of electronic versions of existing printed publications. For the latter it is preferable, wherever possible, to cite the details of original print editions (see also 11.1).

The first example refers to an article in an online encyclopedia:

> Kent Bach, 'Performatives', in *Routledge Encyclopedia of Philosophy* <http://www.rep.routledge.com> [accessed 3 October 2001]

The following is a reference to an individual poem included in a full-text online database:

> E. E. (Edward Estlin) Cummings, 'maggie and milly and molly and may', in *Literature Online* <http://lion.chadwyck.co.uk> [accessed 5 June 2001]

In the final example a complete book of poetry with its original pagination has been included in a database forming part of a larger resource:

Davis McCombs, 'Star Chamber', in *Ultima Thule* (New Haven, CT: Yale University Press, 2000), p. 4, in *Database of Twentieth-Century American Poetry* in *Literature Online* <http://lion.chadwyck.co.uk> [accessed 20 September 2000]

11.2.10.4 OTHER SOURCES

We do not offer guidance here on how to cite references to email correspondence or postings to newsgroups or mailing lists, or to exchanges in multi-user environments, all of which might be regarded as the equivalent of personal written correspondence. Documents on personal Web pages should be used with the caution appropriate to unpublished manuscripts.

For a detailed discussion of how to cite these forms of electronic publication, see Xia Li and Nancy Crane, *Electronic Styles: A Handbook for Citing Electronic Information*, 2nd edn (Medford, NJ: Information Today, 1996) and *International Standard ISO 690-2: 1997* (Geneva: International Organization for Standardization, 1997).

11.2.11 RECORDINGS, FILMS, AND DIGITAL MEDIA

Reference to recordings of music or speech should incorporate the following items, as relevant: composer or author; title of piece and/or compilation, in italics; artist, orchestra, conductor, etc., separated by commas; recording company, CD reference, and date in parentheses.

Ludwig van Beethoven, *Piano Concerto no. 5,* Mitsuko Uchida, Symphonieorchester des Bayerischen Rundfunks, cond. by Kurt Sanderling (Phillips, 462 586-2, 1998).

Ballads of Love and Betrayal, Joglaresa, dir. by Belinda Sykes (Village Life, 01013VL, 2001).

Dylan Thomas, *Under Milk Wood*, read by Anthony Hopkins and Jonathan Pryce (LPF 7667, 1992).

First names of composers, artists, conductors, may be omitted if not deemed necessary.

For films, the reference should include, as a minimum, title, director, distributor, date, e.g.:

The Grapes of Wrath, dir. by John Ford (20th Century Fox, 1940).

Names of artists may be given after that of the director. First names may be omitted if not deemed necessary. If a video reference is available, it should be added at the end.

References to material published on CD or DVD should follow the format outlined in 11.2.1–11.2.3, but with the addition at the end of the phrase '[on CD]', '[on DVD]', etc., as appropriate.

11.3 LATER REFERENCES

In all references to a book or article after the first, the shortest intelligible form should be used. This will normally be the author's name followed by the volume (if applicable) and page reference:

McArthur, p. 62.

Chadwick and Chadwick, III, 72.

Elsky, pp. 42–46 (p. 43).

Sometimes, particularly in the case of editions of 'Works' or collections of essays, a short-title form of reference may be more appropriate:

Boswell, p. 326.

Chaucer, Langland, Arthur, pp. 212–44 (p. 229).

Thomas Nashe, III, 96.

The short title of a multi-author edited collection should be followed by the name(s) of the editor(s):

Susanne Woods, 'The Context of Jonson's Formalism', in *Classic and Cavalier*, ed. by Summers and Pebworth, pp. 77–89.

If no ambiguity is possible, the (volume and) page numbers should be given alone and preferably be included in parentheses within the text rather than as a note (see 10.2). Sometimes it may be necessary, for example when more than one work by an author has been cited, to repeat a title, in a shortened form:

McArthur, *Worlds of Reference*, p. 9.

If there can be no doubt which author is being referred to but more than one of his or her works has been cited, use the short title of the specific work followed by the page reference:

Worlds of Reference, p. 9.

'The Lover as Icarus', p. 12.

The expressions 'loc. cit.' and 'op. cit.' are too vague and should not be used. The term 'ibid.' should be used very sparingly and limited to those situations where there is no possibility of confusion, such as after a second reference which is separated from its predecessor by no more than four lines of typescript.

11.4 CITATION BY THE AUTHOR–DATE SYSTEM

The author–date system requires all bibliographical references to be placed at the end of a book, article, or thesis in alphabetical order by names of author(s) or editor(s), followed by date of publication. The form recommended for use in MHRA publications is as in the following examples:

> Crystal, David. 1992. *An Encyclopedic Dictionary of Language and Languages* (Oxford: Blackwell)

> Macaulay, Donald (ed.). 1992. *The Celtic Languages* (Cambridge: Cambridge University Press)

> Friedland, Jonathan. 2002. 'Across the Divide', *Guardian*, 15 January, section G2, pp. 10–11

> Grady, Hugh. 2001. 'Falstaff: Subjectivity between the Carnival and the Aesthetic', *MLR*, 96: 609–23

In this last example, note the space between the colon and the page reference.

Where there are two or more authors, we recommend the pattern:

> Ogden, C. K., and I. A. Richards

rather than 'Ogden, C. K. and I. A. Richards' or 'Ogden, C. K. and (*or* &) Richards, I. A.'. Editors should be referred to by the abbreviations '(ed.)' or '(eds)'. Note that some non-MHRA journals do not use quotation marks for article titles.

If the list includes more than one work by the same author, a long dash should be substituted for the name after the first appearance and works should be listed in date order, e.g.:

> Posner, Rebecca. 1996. *The Romance Languages* (Cambridge: Cambridge University Press)

> —— 1997. *Linguistic Change in French* (Oxford: Clarendon Press)

If two or more works by the same author(s) have the same publication date, they should be arranged in alphabetical order of title and distinguished by adding letters after the date (e.g. '1998a', '1998b').

References in the text should give in parentheses the surname of the author, the publication date of the work, and, where necessary, a page reference, e.g.:

> Pidgins contrast with creoles, which are created when pidgins acquire native speakers (Crystal 1992: 302).

When the author's name is given in the text, it should not be repeated in the reference. In such cases, the reference either follows the name or, if this seems stylistically preferable, may come at some other point in the same sentence:

> Smith (1977: 66) argues that [...]

Smith, who was known for his contentious views, replied (1977: 66) that
[...]

Smith regards this interpretation as 'wholly unacceptable' (1977: 66).

If original documents are referred to, an abbreviated form of reference
should appear in parentheses in the text and a separate list should appear
at the end of the paper preceding or following the list of published sources
(which may include unpublished theses and dissertations since they have
specific authors). The items in the list should be arranged in systematic
(e.g. alphabetical) order. The following examples illustrate, in the left-hand
column, the abbreviations used in the text and, in the right-hand column,
the full references:

BL MS Cotton Nero A.x.	London, British Library, MS Cotton Nero A.x.
CRO, Probate	Carlisle, Cumberland Record Office, Probate Records
NLS Adv. MS 19.2.1	Edinburgh, National Library of Scotland, Adv. MS 19.2.1
ASV, Cons. X Secr.	Venice, Archivio di Stato, Consiglio dei X, Secreta

11.5 CROSS-REFERENCES

Avoid, as far as possible, cross-references within an article or book. The
page numbers in the printed article or book will not, of course, coincide with
those in the typescript, and numerous references of this kind will therefore
involve considerable extra work for author, editor, and typesetter, and will
increase the possibility of error. Cross-references to pages can sometimes be
avoided by giving references to chapters, sections, or notes, if the notes are
numbered consecutively throughout each chapter or article: 'See Chapter 3',
'See Section 4.3', 'See Chapter 4, n. 7', 'See above at n. 8'.

11.6 BIBLIOGRAPHIES

In an alphabetical bibliography the surname of the author or editor whose
surname governs the alphabetical position will precede the forename(s) or
initial(s). Do not reverse the normal order for collaborating authors or editors
other than the first quoted. The following examples illustrate these points:

Chadwick, H. Munro, and N. Kershaw Chadwick, *The Growth of Literature*,
3 vols (Cambridge: Cambridge University Press, 1932–40; repr. 1986)

Cook, Robert F., '*Baudouin de Sebourc*: un poème édifiant?', *Olifant*, 14
(1989), 115–35

Fuentes, Carlos, *Aura*, ed. by Peter Standish, Durham Modern Language Series: Hispanic Texts, 1 (Durham: University of Durham, 1986)

Johnson, Thomas H., ed., *Emily Dickinson: Selected Letters*, 2nd edn (Cambridge, MA: Harvard University Press, 1985)

McKerrow, Ronald B., ed., *The Works of Thomas Nashe*, 2nd edn, rev. by F. P. Wilson, 5 vols (Oxford: Oxford University Press, 1958)

Strayer, Joseph R., and others, eds, *Dictionary of the Middle Ages,* 13 vols (New York: Scribner, 1982–89), VI (1985)

If the list includes more than one work by the same author, a long dash should be substituted for the name after the first appearance (see 11.4), and the works should be arranged in alphabetical order of title, disregarding initial definite or indefinite articles. Where many of the books cited in the bibliography have the same place of publication (e.g. London or Paris), this may be abbreviated ('L' or 'P') or omitted, but there must be a general note to explain this at the beginning of the bibliography (see 11.2.2 under 7). The titles of frequently cited journals or series should also be abbreviated (without full points) and a list of these and the full forms given in a list of abbreviations:

MLR   *Modern Language Review*

YES   *Yearbook of English Studies*

The system of abbreviations employed in *The Year's Work in Modern Language Studies* is widely used in the fields of language and literature. If the bibliography covers other areas, a system of abbreviations generally recognized within the field should be used.

In a bibliography in list form, final full points after each item should not be used. In a long bibliography of foreign books the native forms of the places of publication are sometimes preferable; and if formal bibliographical descriptions of books are being given, the spelling of the place of publication should be as given on the title page. Whereas the length of an article will be clear from the citation of the first and last page numbers, the length of a book will not, unless the number of pages is stated. Since readers will often need to know whether to expect a pamphlet or a lengthy volume, the number of pages should always be stated in a bibliographical reference work (e.g. *The Year's Work in Modern Language Studies* or a volume in the series Research Bibliographies and Checklists). The number of pages should be stated after the date (or, if the author–date system is used, after the publisher); thus: '238 pp.', or 'xvii + 302 pp.', or '89 pp. + 32 plates', or '130 pp. + CD'. It may also be helpful to include such information in a bibliography placed at the end of a book, article, or thesis.

Whatever system is adopted, it is essential to maintain consistency of styling throughout a bibliography.

PREPARATION OF INDEXES

12.1 GENERAL

Publishers and printers generally expect the index to be submitted on disk or by email. Indexes supplied in hard copy only are unlikely to be acceptable. Indexing facilities within word processors are not generally regarded as satisfactory for compiling anything but the most rudimentary index.

All indexers need technical guidance that is beyond the scope of this *Style Guide*. The Society of Indexers publication *Last but not Least: A Guide for Editors Commissioning Indexes* (http://www.indexers.org.uk/files/lbnl_books.pdf) gives information on the qualities and features that an editor will be looking for in an index.

12.2 INDEX ENTRIES

All scholarly indexes should include subject matter as well as names. It is much easier to compile a name index, but the reader of a book on America in the 1960s who needs to know about mixed marriages or monetary policy, and who finds nothing in the index between 'Miller, Arthur' and 'Monroe, Marilyn', will feel cheated, and with good reason.

Headings with a substantial number of page references should be subdivided: no one wants to look at all thirty-seven pages on which a person is mentioned in order to find the one that gives the date of birth. In general, avoid several levels of indentation, since this would lead to ridiculously short lines in a two-column index. Subentries may often be advantageously grouped in a small block of type. Remember that apparently identical words that have different senses, or represent different parts of speech, must not be grouped in a single entry.

For some types of work (e.g. biographies or critical studies) a single index is normally best. For others (e.g. catalogues of manuscript collections) several indexes may be needed.

One important distinction that experienced indexers make, and that experienced index-users expect, is between substantial treatment of a topic throughout several consecutive pages (shown as e.g. '28–32') and passing references to that topic on each of several consecutive pages (e.g. '28, 29, 30, 31, 32'). Special features such as pages with illustrations or with substantial bibliographical references may be indicated by bold or italic numerals, but such devices should be used sparingly, lest they distract the user. For inclusive numbers, use the convention specified in 8.2, e.g. '301–03' (not '301–3' or '301–303') but '1098–1101' (not '1098–101').

12.3   THE INDEXER

The author of a book may be the best person to index it, but not necessarily so since the author may not be best placed to see it from the reader's point of view. Authors can make good indexers only if they are fully aware of indexing principles and can put them into practice. They may find that the task is more complex and time-consuming than they had realized and that engaging a professional indexer is a better option. In this case, the person engaged should if possible be familiar with the subject-matter of the book.

The Society of Indexers has an online directory, *Indexers Available*, on its website, http://www.indexers.org.uk.

13 PREPARATION OF THESES AND DISSERTATIONS

13.1 GENERAL

There are great variations between universities in their requirements for the presentation and layout of theses. (We use 'thesis' as an inclusive term for both theses and dissertations.) The following general recommendations will be applicable to most theses, but should be supplemented by reference to the particular regulations of the university in which the thesis is to be presented. Candidates must, therefore, be in possession of a current copy of local regulations before a thesis is prepared for presentation.

All theses should be produced on a word processor, even though local regulations may still allow for the presentation of theses produced on a typewriter. In what follows, therefore, the terms 'typing', 'typescript', 'typist', etc. refer to production by word processor. It is also taken for granted that recommendations in earlier parts of this *Style Guide* have been followed.

13.2 LENGTH OF THE THESIS

Local regulations vary considerably on the permitted lengths of theses and these regulations must be consulted and observed. The total length normally refers to the number of words in the main text (including notes) and appendices, but usually excludes preliminary matter, bibliography, and index.

13.3 PARTS OF THE THESIS

13.3.1 TITLE PAGE

The title should be a concise and accurate description of the content of the thesis. The title page should also give the full name of the author, the qualification for which the thesis is submitted, the name of the university in which it is presented, and the date (month and year). Many institutions have a prescribed form of words for the title page, which must be followed. If the thesis is in more than one volume, the number of volumes should be given on the title page of the first volume and later volumes should have their own title pages with the particular volume number specified. Pagination should normally be continuous throughout the volumes.

13.3.2   ABSTRACT OR SYNOPSIS

An abstract should be included even if local regulations do not require it. It is helpful to the reader, and it can be included in such publications as *Dissertation Abstracts International*. Local regulations are often precise and strict about the position, length, and form of the abstract. Unless other regulations apply, it should not exceed five hundred words. An accurate and concise summary of the content and organization of the thesis is normally required. The scope of the work undertaken, the method of investigation, the main divisions of the thesis, and the conclusions reached should all be described. The contribution made by the thesis to knowledge of the subject treated should be clearly stated.

13.3.3   TABLE OF CONTENTS AND LIST OF ILLUSTRATIONS

Any preliminary sections following the table of contents, chapter and appendix numbers and titles, bibliography, and index should all be listed in the table of contents, with page references. Titles must agree exactly with their wording in the main text of the thesis. The listing of smaller subdivisions within chapters is useful, and if the thesis has no index it is essential. Such subheadings should be listed in full, and consistently throughout all chapters and sections. If a thesis is bound in more than one volume, the contents of the whole thesis should be listed in the first volume; each subsequent volume should begin with a list of its own contents.

A list, or lists, of illustrations, diagrams, etc. should follow the table of contents and should also give page references. For any full-page illustration which does not form part of the continuous page numbering of the thesis, this reference should be to the number of the page preceding the item in question.

13.3.4   PREFACE, ACKNOWLEDGEMENTS, DECLARATION

A preface may usefully follow the list of contents. General assistance that you wish to recognize — from supervisors, librarians, colleagues, grant-giving bodies — should be acknowledged here. Acknowledgements of specific instances of assistance are frequently better placed in a note at the relevant point in the text; acknowledgement of permission to reproduce illustrations, quotations, etc. should appear with the material concerned. When a thesis contains material that the author has already published (or used in an earlier thesis), this should be indicated in a preliminary declaration. If the thesis is based on joint research, the nature and extent of the candidate's individual contribution should also be defined here.

13.3.5 List of Abbreviations

Abbreviations (of titles, etc.) regularly used throughout a thesis should be listed, with a key, immediately before the first page of the main text (see also Chapter 4).

13.3.6 Text

Theses should be divided into parts, chapters, sections, and subsections as may be appropriate. The first chapter will normally take the form of an introduction, placing the thesis in relation to its general topic and to other work in the subject. Chapter titles and headings of sections and subsections should be factual, concise, and descriptively accurate.

13.3.7 Notes

Unless local regulations specify otherwise, notes should be numbered in a single sequence throughout each chapter (or section), beginning a new sequence for each chapter, etc. Use the automatic footnote, not the endnote, function of a word processor, where available. It is important to remember that, although a word processor will renumber footnotes automatically, most will not change references in the text (e.g. 'See note 3 above'), and these changes must be made separately by the author. For the placing of note references, see 10.3. Where an automatic noting facility is not available, the note reference numbers within the text should be typed as superior (superscript) figures without punctuation (most automatic noting facilities on word processors will do this automatically). The notes should be prepared in smaller type and single line spacing and placed at the foot of each page. If, in exceptional circumstances, it is impossible to do this, the notes should be placed at the end of each chapter, section, etc.

13.3.8 Appendices

Supporting information that is not suitable for inclusion in the main text or notes may be incorporated in one or more appendices. These could include such material as tables, lists, transcriptions of documentary sources, and descriptions of manuscripts. They should be appropriately titled. They must never be used to include material of doubtful relevance or to avoid the constraints of the official word limit of the thesis (see 13.2).

13.3.9 Bibliography

Every thesis must contain a bibliography, detailing all works referred to in the text (including notes and appendices). It should give full publication details according to the model given in 11.6 (or 11.4 if the author–date system is used).

Some degree of subdivision may be desirable; in particular, manuscript and printed material, and primary and secondary sources, should be distinguished and it may be desirable to provide separate listings for works in different alphabets. Works not specifically referred to should not be included; if necessary, important items not cited in the main text could be mentioned in the introduction and therefore qualify for inclusion. Lists should normally be in alphabetical order by author, unless there is good reason to adopt an alternative order (such as chronological order for primary sources).

While the work is in progress, bibliographical details should be held separately from the thesis drafts, e.g. in computer files or bibliographical databases. If you adopt an author–date bibliography, take care to ensure that the lettering of items of the same date referred to in your text (e.g. 2006a, 2006b) corresponds to that given in the bibliography.

13.3.10 INDEX

Although not always required by local regulations, the provision of an index of names and subjects is highly desirable, particularly for theses covering a wide range of material or concerned with the work of several authors.

13.4 PREPARATION OF THE TYPESCRIPT

13.4.1 GENERAL

Unless local regulations specify otherwise, theses should be printed on one side only of good quality paper. An easily readable typeface, such as 12-point Times New Roman, should be used. Margins should be 4 cm wide at the left-hand side (for binding) and 3 cm on the other three sides.

Double spacing should be used throughout. The bibliography is best presented using a hanging indent for each entry, as in 11.6 above.

Unless local regulations stipulate otherwise, page numbers should begin on the first page of the main text (following the preliminaries) and continue to the end, and should be placed at the top right of each page.

13.4.2 HEADINGS AND SUBHEADINGS

There is a great variety of possible divisions of a thesis: Are the chapters grouped into Parts I, II, etc.? Are the chapters divided into sections? Are there subsections? Is a structured system of numbering used, as in this *Style Guide*? This variety makes it impossible to lay down detailed rules. However, two basic principles must be observed, and both depend on the concept of a hierarchy of divisions (part, chapter, section, subsection, etc.). The first principle is that the hierarchy must be reflected in the space left between units: if there are parts, each part must begin on a new page and should have its own title page; chapters (and equivalent main sections) should always begin on a new page; sections should have more space between them than subsections. The second principle is that of typographical distinction of headings: the heading of a part must be more prominent than that of a chapter, which must be more prominent than that of a section, and so on. Word processors make it easy to centre headings or set them at the left margin, to use larger type, and to use small capitals, italic type, etc. in order to give the appropriate level of prominence. There should be more space between the end of a section and the heading of the next section than between a heading and the section it introduces.

13.4.3 CHECKING AND CORRECTION

The whole text should be thoroughly checked before the final version is printed. Quotations and references should again be checked against the originals (not merely against a previous version), note numbers should be checked, and the typescript should be read through at least once more.

13.4.4 CROSS-REFERENCES

Unless a thesis is divided into small subsections, page numbers will normally be essential for cross-references. These should be kept to a minimum.

13.4.5 ILLUSTRATIONS AND TABLES

If possible, illustrations should be inserted in the thesis near the relevant portion of the text. There should be a separate numbering sequence for each category of illustration (plates, figures, tables, etc.). Numbers and captions should appear below the illustration.

13.4.6 NUMBER OF COPIES

Local regulations vary on the number of copies of a thesis to be presented and on whether one copy is returned to the candidate after the thesis has been examined. All copies, by whatever method they are produced, must be identical.

13.5 BINDING

Nearly every university requires that theses should be bound in boards; some require this binding to be delayed until after the thesis has been examined, others require binding to be completed before submission. Local regulations on the style of binding and on the lettering on the front board (if any) and the spine (usually at least the name of the candidate, the degree, and the year) must be observed.

13.6   PERMISSION TO CONSULT AND COPY

Many universities require the authors of theses deposited in their libraries to sign a declaration granting to the librarian the right to permit, without further reference to the author, consultation of the thesis and the making of single copies (for study purposes, and subject to the usual conventions of scholarly acknowledgement) of all or of parts of it. As always it is essential to be aware of current regulations in the institution to which the thesis is being submitted.

13.7   FURTHER READING

The following may be found useful:

Barzun, Jacques, and Henry F. Graff, *The Modern Researcher*, 6th edn (Belmont, CA: Thomson/Wadsworth, 2004)

Murray, Rowena, *How to Write a Thesis*, 2nd edn (Maidenhead: Open University Press, 2006)

Oliver, Paul, *Writing your Thesis* (London: SAGE, 2004)

USEFUL WORKS OF REFERENCE

BS ISO 999: 1996: Information and Documentation. Guidelines for the Content, Organization and Presentation of Indexes (London: British Standards Institution, 1996)

BS 5261-1: 2000: Copy Preparation and Proof Correction. Design and Layout of Documents (London: British Standards Institution, 2000)

Butcher, Judith, Caroline Drake, and Maureen Leach, *Butcher's Copy-Editing: The Cambridge Handbook for Editors, Copy-Editors and Proofreaders*, 4th edn (Cambridge: Cambridge University Press, 2006)

The Chicago Manual of Style, 15th edn (Chicago and London: University of Chicago Press, 2003)

Gibaldi, Joseph, *MLA Handbook for Writers of Research Papers*, 6th edn (New York: Modern Language Association of America, 2003)

—— *MLA Style Manual and Guide to Scholarly Publishing*, 2nd edn (New York: Modern Language Association of America, 1998)

Li, Xia, and Nancy Crane, *Electronic Styles: A Handbook for Citing Electronic Information*, 2nd edn (Medford, NJ: Information Today, 1996)

Merriam-Webster's Concise Handbook for Writers, 2nd edn (Springfield, MA: Merriam-Webster, 1998)

Ritter, R. M., Angus Stevenson, and Lesley Brown, *New Oxford Dictionary for Writers and Editors: The Essential A–Z Guide to the Written Word* (Oxford: Oxford University Press, 2005)

Ritter, Robert, *The Oxford Style Manual* (Oxford: Oxford University Press, 2003)

PROOF CORRECTION

It is common for proofs to be emailed as PDF files rather than sent as hard copy. The author should consult with the editor whether proofs should be printed off and changes marked on the hard copy, or whether they may be communicated in a list in a separate email.

Make all corrections distinctly in ink in the margins; marks made in the text should be those indicating the place to which the correction refers and should not obliterate the text to be corrected. An alteration is made by striking through, or marking as indicated in the table below, the character, word(s), to be altered, and writing the new material in the margin, followed by a concluding stroke (/). If several corrections occur in one line they should be divided between left and right margins, the order being from left to right in each margin; individual marks should be separated by a concluding stroke. Author corrections should be avoided at proof stage. However, if such changes are essential, authors should be aware that substantial additions or deletions will affect layout and pagination and the editor may insist on further changes within the page to compensate for the text added or deleted. Publishers and journals may reserve the right to charge for substantial changes.

When checking final proofs, ensure not only that each correction marked on earlier proofs has been made, but also that no further errors have been introduced during the process of correction. Check line endings, page breaks, running heads, and page numbers carefully. It is safer to check these points as a separate operation after reading through the proofs in the normal way.

Normally only matter to be substituted for, or added to, the existing text should be written on the proof. If, however, there are any problems or comments to be brought to the attention of the printer, they should be written on the proof, encircled, and preceded by the word 'PRINTER' (in capitals). Do not give lengthy directions to the printer when a simple proof-correction mark will suffice.

The following table of proof-correction marks is based on Part 2 of *BS5261: Marks for Copy Preparation and Proof Correction* (London: British Standards Institution, 2005) and material from this publication is reproduced by permission of the British Standards Institution, 389 Chiswick High Road, London W4 4AL, UK (tel.: +44 (0) 208 996 9000), from whom complete copies may be obtained.

NOTE The letters M and P in the notes column indicate marks for marking up copy and for correcting proofs respectively.

Group A: General

No.	Instruction	Textual mark	Marginal mark	Notes
A1	End of change	None	/ or solidus followed by a circled number bottom right /⊗	P Make after every change that is not an insertion or deletion, i.e. followed by B1 (This is identical to B4) Use circled number to indicate number of times same change is repeated in the same line without interruption
A2	Leave unchanged	— — — — — under characters to remain	Ⓥ	M P
A3	Push down risen spacing material	Circle blemish	⊥	P For hot metal only
A4	Refer to appropriate authority anything of doubtful accuracy	Circle word(s) affected	(?)	P

Group B: Deletion, insertion and substitution

| B1 | Insert in text the matter indicated in the margin | ⋀ | New matter followed by
 ⋀
 or
 ⋀⊗ | M P
 Use circled number to indicate number of times same insert is repeated in the same line without interruption |
| B2 | Insert additional matter identified by a letter in a diamond | ⋀ | ⋀
 preceded by, for example,
 ◇A◇ | M P
 The relevant section of the copy should be supplied with the corresponding letter marked on it in a diamond, e.g. ◇A◇ |

Table 1 — Classified list of marks (*continued*)

No.	Instruction	Textual mark	Marginal mark	Notes
B3	Delete	/ through single character, rule or underline or ⊢———⊣ through all characters to be deleted	M P Use for deletion at the beginning or end of a word and where no space is to be left in place of deletion. Use circled number to indicate number of deletions in the same line without interruption
B4	Substitute character or substitute part of one or more word(s)	/ through character or ⊢———⊣ through all characters	new character / or new characters /	M P
B5	Wrong font. Replace by character(s) of correct font	Circle character(s) to be changed		P Use to indicate wrong typeface or size
B6	Change damaged character(s) or remove extraneous marks	Circle character(s) to be changed or mark(s) to be removed	✕	P
B7	Set in or change to italic	under character(s) to be set or changed		M P Where space does not permit textual marks, or for clarity, circle the affected area instead
B8	Change italic to roman/vertical type	Circle character(s) to be changed		M P
B9	Set in or change to bold type	～～～ under character(s) to be set or changed	～	M P Where space does not permit textual marks, or for clarity, circle the affected area instead
B10	Change bold to non-bold type	Circle character(s) to be changed		M P
B11	Set in or change to bold italic type	～～～ under character(s) to be set or changed		M P Where space does not permit textual marks, or for clarity, circle the affected area instead

No.	Instruction	Textual mark	Marginal mark	Notes
B12	Change to non-bold and non-italic	Circle character(s) to be changed		M P
B13	Set in or change to capital letters	under character(s) to be set or changed		M P Where space does not permit textual marks, or for clarity, circle the affected area instead
B14	Set in or change to small capital letters	under character(s) to be set or changed		
B15	Set in or change to capital letters for initial letters and small capital letters for the rest of the words	under initial letters and under rest of words		
B16	Change capital letters to lower case letters	Circle character(s) to be changed		P
B17	Change small capital letters to lower case letters	Circle character(s) to be changed		P
B18	Turn type or figure	Circle type or figure to be altered		P Use circled number to give number of degrees of rotation, e.g. 180
B19	Substitute or insert character in 'superior' position	/ through character or ∧ where required	under character e.g.	P Do not use additional insert or substitute mark with these marks
B20	Substitute or insert character in 'inferior' position	/ through character or ∧ where required	over character e.g.	
B21	Substitute ligature, e.g. ffi, for separate letters	through characters affected	e.g. ffi	P
B22	Substitute separate letters for ligature	through characters affected	Write out separate letters	P

No.	Instruction	Textual mark	Marginal mark	Notes
B23	Substitute or insert full stop or decimal point	/ through character or ∧ where required	⊙	M P
B24	Substitute or insert colon	/ through character or ∧ where required	⊙	M P
B25	Substitute or insert semi-colon	/ through character or ∧ where required	;	M P
B26	Substitute or insert comma	/ through character or ∧ where required	,	M P
B27	Substitute or insert apostrophe	/ through character or ∧ where required	⸤ or ⸥	M P Do not use additional insert or substitute mark with these marks
B28	Substitute or insert single quotation marks	/ through character or ∧ where required	⸤ or ⸥ and/or ⸤ or ⸥	
B29	Substitute or insert double quotation marks	/ through character or ∧ where required	⸤⸤ or ⸥⸥ and/or ⸤⸤ or ⸥⸥	
B30	Substitute or insert ellipsis or leader dots	/ through character or ∧ where required	⊙⊙⊙	M P When used as leader, give the measure
B31	Substitute or insert hyphen	/ through character or space or ∧ where required	⊢-⊣	M P

Licensed to MHRA under licence number 2007JK0046 ©BSI

No.	Instruction	Textual mark	Marginal mark	Notes
B32	Substitute or insert rule	/ through character or ⋀ where required	⊢	M P Give the size of the rule in the margin mark e.g.
B33	Substitute or insert oblique	/ through character or ⋀ where required	⊘	M P
B34	Insert underline	Circle characters/words	Circle horizontal line	M P

Group C: Positioning

No.	Instruction	Textual mark	Marginal mark	Notes
C1	Start new paragraph			M P
C2	Run on (no new paragraph, no new line)			M P
C3	Transpose characters or words	between characters or words		M P
C4	Transpose a number of characters or words	③ ② ①	① ② ③	M P Use when the sequence cannot be clearly indicated by the use of C3 Circle numbers to prevent them being typeset
C5	Transpose lines			M P Extend rules the full length of matter being transposed
C6	Transpose a number of lines	③ ② ①		P Use when the sequence cannot be clearly indicated by the use of C5 Circle numbers to prevent them being typeset

No.	Instruction	Textual mark	Marginal mark	Notes
C7	Centre	enclosing matter to be centred		M P
C8	Indent or move beginning of line(s) to the right			M P Draw vertical lines of mark to show position to which character(s) are moved
C9	Cancel indent or move end of line(s) to the left			
C10	Set line justified to specified measure	and/or		P Give the exact dimensions when necessary
C11	Set column justified to specified measure			M P Give the exact dimensions when necessary
C12	Unjustify		or	M P Use mark on side of line/column to be unjustified
C13	Move specified matter to the right	enclosing matter to be moved to the right		P Draw vertical line to show position to which matter is moved
C14	Move specified matter to the left	enclosing matter to be moved to the left		
C15	Take over character(s), word(s) or line to next line, column or page			P The textual mark surrounds the matter to be taken over and extends into the margin

No.	Instruction	Textual mark	Marginal mark	Notes
C16	Take back character(s), word(s), or line to previous line, column or page			P The textual mark surrounds the matter to be taken back and extends into the margin
C17	Raise matter	over matter to be raised under matter to be raised		P Give the exact dimensions when necessary (Use D8 for insertion of space between lines or paragraphs in text)
C18	Lower matter	over matter to be lowered under matter to be lowered		P Give the exact dimensions when necessary (Use D9 for reduction of space between lines or paragraphs in text)
C19	Move matter to position indicated	Enclose matter to be moved and indicate new position		P Give the exact dimensions when necessary
C20	Correct vertical alignment			P
C21	Correct horizontal alignment	Single line above and below misaligned matter e.g. misaligned		P The marginal mark is placed level with the head and foot of the relevant line

Group D: Spacing

No.	Instruction	Textual mark	Marginal mark	Notes
D1	Close up. Delete space between characters or words	linking characters		M P
D2	Insert or substitute space between characters or words	through character or where required		M P Give the size of the space to be inserted when necessary

No.	Instruction	Textual mark	Marginal mark	Notes
D3	Reduce space between characters or words	| between characters or words affected	⌐	M P Give amount by which the space is to be reduced when necessary
D4	Make space equal between characters or words in entire line	| between characters or words affected	⅄	M P
D5	Insert or substitute thin space	/ through character or ⋀ where required	♀	M P
D6	Insert or substitute fixed space	/ through character or ⋀ where required	(2pt) ⵏ or ⵏ	M P Circle numbers to prevent them being typeset
D7	Close up to normal interline spacing		(each side of column linking lines)	M P The marks are in the margin
D8	Insert space between lines or paragraphs	⌐ or ⌐		M P The mark extends between the lines of text. Give the size of the space to be inserted when necessary
D9	Reduce space between lines or paragraphs	⊃ or ⊂		M P The mark extends between the lines of text. Give the amount by which the space is to be reduced when necessary

Marked proof of text

(B15) ＝/
(D1) ◡/

'A Provisional Hypothesis': Paternity or Pangenesis?   Ƴ/ (D2)

by Ashley Taggart

In this article I examine August Strindberg's play The Father   └┘/ (B7)
(1887) in relation to a particular biological debate current at the
time. To do so, it is first necessary to place this work within a
movement, naturalism, which self-consciously allied itself with
'new' evolutionary evelopments. After all, only nine months after
the premiere of The Father Strindberg is able to write, in a letter   ⌐┘/ (B8)
to Karl Bonnier of August 1888: 'Keep your tongue straight in
your mouth, for now naturalism is entering the academy (not the
Swedish); and it will never be superseded as a philosophy until
(B32) Darwinism whose logical consequence it is — is abandoned: Hoc
(B24) est never!'. For him, naturalism marks a radical break with the
past. Moreover, its fate as a literary movement is indissolubly
linked to the theories of Charles Darwin. Should Darwinism be
discredited, then naturalism, 'whose logical consequence it is',
(C3) necessarily would fall in its wake.
It is worth stating at the outset what an extraordinary aesthetic   ⌐/ (C8)
stance this is. Strindberg espouses evolution for better or worse,
appending the fate of naturalism to an entirely scientific
breakthrough. However, the tone of this and other avowals attests
to his fervent belief that there is no question of 'worse', and that
with Darwinism he has found, in Zola's words, 'the instrument of
(C1) my epoch'. Paradoxically, those very qualities that made
Strindberg a brilliant theatrical innovator (readiness to assimilate
new ideas, the ability to immerse himself completely in the latest'
discipline, a fearsome subjectivity) made him a poor Prophet. The   ≠/ (B16)
day would come when he would feel himself quite capable of
abandoning naturalism and denouncing 'Father Darwin and his
son Haeckel', for reasons that lay well outside the sphere of
'logic', 'philosophy', or scientific rebuttal. To complete this last
(B28) quotation: 'Father Darwin and his son Haeckel knew nothing and
wished to know nothing about the resurrection; they only knew
(B28) about birth and death.' So pronounced is the later Strindberg's   ⅂/ (B19)
disgust that he gives way to wild fulmination on what he now sees
as the glaring absurdities of evolutionary theory. However, at the
time of writing The Father this violent volte face lay many years
in the future, and Strindberg remained a committed follower of
(B23) Darwin/

(D3) ⊤

(826) ,/

(83) ⌒

His naturalistic plays, of which *The Father* is an early example, embody a range of attitudes to the revelations of *The Origin of Species*. Characters are given speeches which quite simply could not ⎮ have ⎮ been ⎮ written ⎮ in ⎮ a ⎮ pre-evolutionary ⎮ context. ⎮ It is not simply that they have overtones of Darwinian 'struggle', or the battle of wills. Beyond this, the playwright sets up oppositions/ like that between Miss Julie and her servant, Jean, which take much of their symbolic force from a dialectic within evolutionary thought. How far sheer strength of will can make one stronger in the fight to survive is, and was then, question/ able. Can psychological toughness and adaptability and

adaptability raise a humble species from its origins, or is it for

ever condemned by an inferior genetic heritage? Or, to translate

this into the language of class, can aspiration and intelligence ever

be enough to transcend caste barriers?

of (83)

≠/ (817)

⊢ (831)

(D7)

(+ 2pts (D8)

(89) ∾
(C14) ⊐/

(813) ≡/

Paternity
Strindberg taps into a debate between the Lamarkian evolutionists, who believe that intention/ and the hard-line geneticists, who saw it all as a matter of physical (genetic) endowment. In order to understand the opposing forces embodied in *The Father*, it is first of all necessary to look briefly at the development of darwin's relationship with Lamarck, and to remember that for Strindberg, writing in the 1800s, the key issues of transmutation, differentiation, reversion, and struggle were far from settled, and retained the power to disturb and outrage.

c/ (81)
Ⓐ/ (82)

(?) (A4)

(- 2pts (D8)

¹ *A Blue Book*, trans. by Claud Field (London: Allen, 1913), p. 223.

Ⓐ and volition have a role in elevating even the 'lowest' organisms to greater complexity,

INDEX

References are to sections

abbreviations 4
  American states 4.5, 11.2.2
  capitalized 4.4
  currency 8.4
  editors 11.4
  endnotes 4.3
  footnotes 4.3
  full point 4.4, 9.3
  italics 7.2
  journal titles 11.2.4, 11.6
  manuscript references 11.2.9
  postal 4.5
  quotations 2.4
  references 11.1, 11.2.1, 11.2.2, 11.3
  titles 4.2
  weights and measures 8.5
abbreviations list 11.2.4
  glossary 1.5
  theses 13.3.5
  titles 11.6
abstract, thesis 13.3.2
academic qualifications 6.7
accents
  capitals 6.6
  see also diacritics
acceptance for publication 1.2.1
accounts, numbers in columns 8.2
acknowledgements 1.3.12, 1.5
  thesis 13.3.4
additions 1.3.2.2
adjectives, capitalized 6.1
adverbs, hyphenation 2.3
alphabets 1.3.3, 1.3.10
amendments, minor 1.3.1
American states 4.5
  abbreviated names 11.2.2
American universities 11.2.6
angle brackets 5.3, 11.2.10.1
anthology of criticism 11.1
apostrophe 2.5

truncations 2.6
appendix 1.5, 10.1
  thesis 13.3.8
arabic numerals 8.3
  Bible references 11.2.8
  journal volume numbers 11.2.4
  lines of poems 11.2.7
Arabic script 1.3.10
art, works of 7.4
articles
  cross-references 11.5
  journals 11.2.4
  magazines 11.2.5
  newspapers 11.2.5
  online publications 11.2.10.2
  references 11.1, 11.2.3
  type for titles 7.3
asterisk, general note to chapter 10.3
author–date system citations 11.4, 13.3.9
author-typeset formats 1.4, 1.5
authors
  bibliography 11.6
  collaborating 11.6
  corrections 1.3.2.2, 15
  final copy design 1.3.1
  indexing 12.3
  multiple 11.4
  name in text 11.4
  online publications 11.2.10.1
  references to books 11.2.2, 11.2.3
  references to journals 11.2.4
  responsibilities 1.2.3
  retained copy 1.3.1
  revisions 1.3.2.2
  typesetting 1.5
author's preface 1.5

Bible
  references 11.2.8
  titles of books 7.3
bibliographical descriptions 2.4
bibliographical details 1.5

bibliographical references
  abbreviations 4.4
  author–date system 11.4, 13.3.9
  indexing 12.2
  bibliography 1.5, 11.6
  explanatory note 11.6
  note limiting 10.2
  number of pages 11.6
  spacing 13.4.1
  thesis 13.3.9, 13.4.1
bold type 1.3.3
books
  alternative titles 11.2.2
  cross-references 11.5
  online database 11.2.10.3
  order of parts 1.5
  references 11.2.2, 11.2.3
  subdivisions 11.2.3
  titles 6.4, 7.3, 11.4
  type for titles 7.3
  volume numbers 8.3
braces 5.3
brackets 5.3
*BS5261: Marks for Copy Preparation and
  Proof Correction* (2005) 15

camera-ready copy (CRC) 1.4.3, 1.5
capitals 1.3.3, 1.3.15, 6
  accented 6.6
  book titles 6.4
  dignities 6.2
  foreign titles 6.4
  hyphenated compounds 6.5
  initial 6.1
  journal titles 6.4
  large 1.3.3
  movements 6.3
  periods 6.3
  prehistoric eras 6.5
  quotations 9.1
  references 11.2.2, 11.2.4
  small 1.3.3, 1.3.15, 6.7, 8.1, 8.3
  subtitles 6.4
  titles of people 6.2
  titles of writings 6.4
  unpublished theses/dissertations 11.2.6
captions to illustrations 1.3.12, 13.4.5
CD-ROM references 11.2.11
Celtic names 3.3.1
centuries 8.1

small capitals 8.3
chapter
  general note 10.3
  references 11.2.3
  thesis 13.3.6
chapter titles
  camera-ready copy 1.4.3.2
  references 11.2.3
  roman type 7.3
  thesis 13.3.6
checking of typescript
  final version 1.2.3, 15
  thesis 13.4.3
Chinese script 1.3.10
classical names 3.3.2.1
colons 1.3.9, 5.2
  references 11.2.2, 11.2.3, 11.2.4
commas 5.1, 5.2
  numbers 8.2
  quotation marks 9.3
comments
  for editor 1.3.2.2
  for printers 9.4, 9.5, 15
  for typesetter 1.3.2.2
compound words 2.3
compounds 5.5
conjunctions 11.2.2
contents list 1.5
  thesis 13.3.3
copy preparation 1.3
  typing 1.3.2
copyright 1.5
  quotations 9.7
corrections
  marking 1.3.2.2
  see also proof correction
criticism, anthology 11.1
cross-references 1.3.14, 11.5
  theses 13.4.4
currency 8.4
Cyrillic alphabet 1.3.10, 3.3.2.2
Cyrillic script, roman numerals 8.3

dashes 1.3.5, 5.2
  long 11.4
databases
  bibliographical 13.3.9
  online 11.2.10.3
dates 8.1, 8.2
  journals 11.2.4

newspapers/magazines 11.2.5
online publications 11.2.10.1, 11.2.10.2
decades 8.1
declaration in thesis 13.3.4
dedication 1.5
definite article
    journal title 11.2.4
    newspaper title 11.2.5
    place names 3.1.1, 3.1.2
desktop publishing (DTP) software 1.4.2,
    1.5
diacritics 1.3.10, 2.2
    see also accents
dictionaries 2.2, 2.3, 6.1
    biographical 11.1
digital images 1.3.12
digital media references 11.2.11
Digital Object Identifier (DOI) 11.2.10.1,
    11.2.10.2
dignities 6.2
disks 1.2.2
    references 11.2.11
Dissertation Abstracts International
    13.3.2
dissertations
    preparation 13
    published extract 11.2.6
    references 11.2.6, 11.4
    see also theses
ditto 5.2
divisions, hierarchy of 13.4.2
dollars 8.4
double-spacing 1.3.2.1, 1.3.9, 13.4.1
drawings 1.3.12
DVD-ROM references 11.2.11

email attachments 1.2.2
editions
    original 11.1
    references 11.1, 11.2.2
editors
    abbreviation 11.4
    bibliography 11.6
    comments for 1.3.2.2
    indexes 12.1
    instructions to typesetter 1.3.1
    references 11.2.2
electronic publications 11.2.10
electronic submission 1.4.2
ellipses 5.7

omissions within quotations 9.6
2-em dash 1.3.5, 5.2
em rule 1.3.5, 5.2
en rule 1.3.5, 5.2
encyclopedias, references to 11.1
endnotes 1.3.11, 10.1
    abbreviations 4.3
era citations 8.1
essay titles 7.3
    references 11.2.3
expository material 10.1

facsimile reprint references 11.1, 11.2.2
figures (numerical) 8.2
figures in text 1.3.12
    numbering 13.4.5
file transfer to printers 1.4.2
films
    references 11.2.11
    titles 7.4
final version 1.2.1
    avoidance of over-design 1.3.1
    checking 1.2.3, 15
    revised 1.2.3
footnotes 1.3.11, 10.1
    abbreviations 4.3
    checking 13.4.3
    references 11.1
    word-processor function 13.3.7
foreign expressions 2.2
foreign language
    currency 8.4
    italics 7.2
    quotations/quotation marks 9.2
    roman numerals 8.3
foreign-language characters 1.3.10
    accents on capitals 6.6
foreign names 3.3.2
    place names 3.1
    Slavonic 3.3.2.2
foreign titles 6.4
foreign words in italics 7.2
foreword 1.5
fonts 1.3.3
    see also type size; typeface
full point
    abbreviations 4.4
    long quotations 9.4
    notes 10.1
    parentheses 5.3

quotation marks 9.3
quotations 9.3
references 11.2.7, 11.2.8
short quotations 9.3

Greek alphabet 1.3.10

half-title 1.5
hard copy 1.3.1
    annotation 1.3.1
    cross-references 1.3.14
    special characters 1.3.10
    tables 1.3.13
headings 1.3.1, 1.3.4
    camera-ready copy 1.4.3
    compounds 6.5
    punctuation 5.4
    section 13.3.6
    thesis 13.4.2
    typographical distinctions 13.4.2
    word processors 13.4.2
Hebrew script 1.3.10
hyphens 1.3.5, 1.3.9, 2.3
    place names 3.1.1

illustrations 1.3.12
    indexing 12.2
    list 1.5, 13.3.3
    numbering 13.4.5
    permission 9.7
    thesis 13.3.3, 13.4.5
indefinite article
    journal title 11.2.4
    newspaper title 11.2.5
indents 1.3.2.1
    quotations 9.4, 9.5
index 1.5, 12
    entries 12.2
    features 12.1
    page references 12.2
    qualities 12.1
    subentries 12.2
    submission 12.1
    thesis 13.3.10
indexers, professional 12.3
Indexers Available 12.3
Internet publications 11.2.10.1
introduction 1.5
italics/italic type 1.3.3, 7
    copy produced on typewriter 1.3.15

foreign expressions 2.2
foreign words 7.2
journal titles 11.2.4
punctuation 5.5
quotations 9.1
stage directions 9.5
titles 7.3, 7.4

Japanese script 1.3.10
journal titles 6.4, 7.3, 11.4
    abbreviations 11.2.4, 11.6
    references 11.2.3, 11.2.4
journals
    article references 11.2.3, 11.2.4, 11.4
    page numbers 11.2.4
    publication date 11.2.4
    volume numbers 11.2.4
justification 1.3.2.1, 1.3.9

Koran 7.3

Last but not Least: A Guide for Editors Commissioning Indexes 12.1
Latin words 7.2
learned society proceedings 11.2.4
legal case citation 7.3
letters, references to 11.1
Library of Congress system 3.3.2.2
line division for quotations of verse 9.3
line ends
    camera-ready copy 1.4.3.2
    checking 15
line spacing 1.3.2.1
    double 1.3.2.1, 13.4.1
    theses 13.4.1
literary works
    references 11.1, 11.2.4
    title abbreviations 4.2
    titles within article titles 11.2.4

magazine article references 11.2.5
manuscripts
    references 11.2.9
    typing 13.4.1
margins
    proof corrections 15
    theses 13.4.1
measurement 8.5
The Modern Language Review 3.3.2.2
monarchs 3.3.2.1

roman numerals 8.3
money 8.4
Moslem *see* Muslim
movements 6.3
Muhammad 3.3.2.1
multi-volume work references 11.2.2
musical composition titles 7.4
Muslim 3.3.2.1

names 3
  indexes 12.2
  references 11.2.2
  see also personal names; place names
newspaper article references 11.2.5
non-alphabetic scripts 1.3.10
notes 1.3.11, 1.5, 10.1
  checking 13.4.3
  general to chapter 10.3
  limiting 10.2
  numbering 1.3.11, 9.3, 12.3.7, 12.4.1, 12.4.6
  position 9.3, 12.3.7
  references 9.2
  thesis 12.3.7, 12.4.1
  typescript 9.3
  unnumbered 9.3
  see also endnotes; footnotes
numbering
  notes 1.3.11, 10.3, 13.3.7
  pages 1.3.1, 1.3.8
  preliminary pages 1.5
  subdivisions 1.3.4
  text 1.5
numbers 8.2, 8.3
  see also arabic numerals; roman numerals

omissions from quotations 9.6
online publications 11.2.10
  articles 11.2.10.2
  databases 11.2.10.3
  references 11.2.10
order of parts of book 1.5
ordinals 8.1, 8.2
  roman numerals 8.3

page ends for camera-ready copy 1.4.3.2
page numbering 1.3.1, 1.3.8
page numbers
  checking 15

indexes 12.2
journals 11.2.4
  references 11.2.2, 11.2.3
  theses 13.3.1, 13.4.1
paper size 1.3.1
  camera-ready copy 1.4.3.2
paperback reissues, references 11.1
paragraphs 1.3.2.1
parentheses 5.2, 5.3
  punctuation 9.3
  references 9.3, 9.4, 10.2
  roman 9.5
  volume numbers 11.2.2
PDF files 1.4.3.2
periods 6.3
permissions
  acknowledgements 1.3.12
  quotations 9.7
  thesis consultation/copying 13.6
personal names 3.3
  extensions 6.2
  possessive 2.5.2
  Slavonic 3.3.2.2
  substitutes 6.2
phonetic symbols 1.3.10
photographs 1.3.12
place names 3.1
  of publication in references 11.2.2
plates 1.3.12
  numbering 13.4.5
plays
  acts 8.3, 11.2.7
  quotations 9.5
  references 11.2.7
plurals
  foreign currency 8.4
  weights and measures 8.5
poems
  line numbers 11.2.7
  long 11.2.7
  online database 11.2.10.3
  permission 9.7
  references 11.2.7
  subdivisions 8.3
  titles 7.3
  see also verse
popes 2.7
  roman numerals 3.3.2.1
possessive, use of 2.5
postal abbreviations 4.5

postal codes 6.7
PostScript 1.4.3.2
preface
 book 1.5
 thesis 13.3.4
prehistoric eras 6.5
preliminary pages 1.5
 numbering 1.5
 roman numerals 8.3
printers
 file transfer 1.4.2
 marks for 15
printing, camera-ready copy 1.4.3.1
professional qualifications 6.7
proof correction 15
 marking 1.3.2.2
proof marks after reading 15
proof-reading conventions 1.3.2.2, 15
prose quotations
 long 9.4
 omissions from 9.6
 from plays 9.5
 short 9.3
publication details 11.1, 11.2.2
 date 11.2.2, 11.2.4, 11.2.5, 11.4
 online publications 11.2.10.1
 place 11.2.2, 11.6
publishers
 code specifications 1.3.10
 copyright 9.7
 name in references 11.2.2
punctuation 5
 dates 8.1
 ellipses 5.7
 headings 5.4
 italics 5.5
 journal title abbreviations 11.2.4
 long quotations 9.4
 marks 1.3.4, 1.3.9
 note reference numbers 10.3
 notes 10.1
 numbers 8.2
 parentheses 9.3
 quotation marks 9.3
 quotations 9.1, 9.3, 9.4, 9.5
 references 11.2.2, 11.2.3, 11.2.7, 11.2.8
 short quotations 9.3
 see also individual punctuation marks

quotation marks 1.3.6, 7.1, 7.2, 9.1

double 9.3
foreign language 9.2
full point 9.3
long quotations 9.4
poem titles 7.4
punctuation 9.3
references 11.2.2, 11.2.3
song titles 7.4
titles in books/journals 7.3, 11.4
titles within italicized titles 5.5
unpublished theses/dissertations 11.2.6
quotations 2.4, 9.1, 9.4
checking 1.2.3, 13.4.3
copyright 9.7
direct 9.1
foreign language 9.2
indents 9.4
long 9.4, 9.5
mark to typesetter 9.4, 9.5
omissions 9.6
plays 9.5
prose 9.3, 9.4, 9.5, 9.6
punctuation 9.1, 9.3, 9.4, 9.5
within quotation 9.3
short 9.3
spelling 2.4, 9.1, 9.5
thesis 13.4.3
verse 9.3, 9.4, 9.5, 9.6

readers 1.3.1
proof marks 15
recordings, references 11.2.11
referees 1.3.1
proof marks 15
reference works 14
references 1.5, 11.1
abbreviated form 11.1, 11.2.1, 11.4
abbreviations 4.4
articles 11.2.3
articles in journals 11.2.4
author–date system 11.4, 13.3.9
Bible 11.2.8
books 11.2.2, 11.2.3
capitalization 11.2.2, 11.2.4
chapters 11.2.3
checking 1.2.3, 13.4.3
digital media 11.2.11
dissertations 11.2.6, 11.4
editions 11.1
electronic publications 11.2.10

films 11.2.11
forms 11.2
indexing 12.2
journals 11.2.3
later 11.3
magazine articles 11.2.5
manuscripts 11.2.9
newspaper articles 11.2.5
notes 10.2
numbers 1.3.11
online publications 11.2.10
page numbers 11.2.2, 11.2.3
parentheses 5.3, 9.3, 9.4, 10.2
plays 11.2.7
poems 11.2.7
publication date 11.2.2, 11.2.4, 11.2.5,
   11.4
publication place 11.2.2, 11.6
publishers 11.2.2
punctuation 11.2.2, 11.2.3, 11.2.4,
   11.2.7, 11.2.8
quotation marks 11.2.2
recordings 11.2.11
simple 10.2
in text 11.4
thesis 11.2.6, 11.4, 13.3.9, 13.4.3
unpublished documents 11.4
well-known works 11.1
see also bibliographies; cross-
   references; publication details
renumbering 1.3.8
reprints, references to 11.1, 11.2.2
research, joint 13.3.4
revisions 1.2.1, 1.2.3, 1.3.2.2
roman numerals 8.3
   acts of plays 11.2.7
   Bible references 11.2.8
   volume numbers 6.7, 11.2.2
roman type
   quotations 7.2
   titles 7.3, 7.4, 11.2.6
round brackets 5.3
running heads 1.3.7
   checking 15
Russian names 3.3.2.2

saints 3.3.2.1
scripts 1.3.10
section headings 13.3.6
semicolons 1.3.9

series references 11.2.2
series titles 11.2.2
short story titles 7.3
The Slavonic and East European Review
   1.2.1, 3.3.2.2
Slavonic names 3.3.2.2
small capitals 1.3.3, 1.3.15, 6.7
   centuries 8.3
   era citations 8.1
smart quotes 1.3.6
Society of Indexers 12.1, 12.3
song titles 7.4
sources, citation 10.1, 10.2
spacing, see line spacing
special characters 1.3.10
spelling 2
   preferred 2.1
   quotations 2.4, 9.1, 9.5
square brackets 5.3
   ellipses 5.7
   journal year of publication 11.2.4
   quotations 9.4
stage directions 9.5
statistical works 8.4, 8.5
style, preferred 1.2.1
style books/sheets 1.2.1
sub-editors 1.2.1
subdivisions 1.3.4
subheadings
   punctuation 5.4
   thesis 13.4.2
   typographic treatment 6.7
submission of copy 1.1
   on disk 1.2.2
   email attachment 1.2.2
   electronic 1.4.2
   initial 1.3.1
subtitles 6.4
synopsis of thesis 13.3.2

tab characters 1.3.2.1
tables 1.3.13
   numbering 13.4.5
   of numbers 8.2
   permission 9.7
   statistical 8.4
   theses 13.4.5
Talmud 7.3
text 1.5
   author's name 11.4

formatting 1.3.9
major subdivisions 8.3
marked proof 15
minor subdivisions 8.3
numbering 1.5
references 11.1, 11.4
thesis 13.3.6
theses
bibliography 13.3.9
binding 13.5
checking/correction 13.4.3
contribution to joint research 13.3.4
cross-references 13.4.4
headings 13.4.2
hierarchy of divisions 13.4.2
illustrations 13.4.5
index 13.3.10
length 13.2, 13.3.8
local regulations 13.1, 13.2, 13.4.6, 13.5
margins 13.4.1
material already published 13.3.4
number of copies 13.4.6
page numbers 13.4.4
paper 13.4.1
parts 13.3
permission to consult/copy 13.6
preparation 13
published extract 11.2.6
quotations 13.4.3
references 11.2.6, 11.4, 13.3.9, 13.4.3
spacing 13.4.1
tables 13.4.5
text 13.3.6
typeface 13.4.1
typescript 13.4
unpublished 7.3, 11.2.6, 11.4
word limit 13.2
title page 1.5
thesis 13.3.1
titles 6.2
abbreviations 4.2, 11.2.4, 11.6, 13.3.5
alternative 11.2.2
within article titles of literary works
11.2.4
books 6.4, 7.3, 11.2.2, 11.4
capitals 6.2, 6.4
chapter 1.4.3.2, 7.3, 11.2.3, 13.3.6
descriptive 7.4
essay 7.3, 11.2.3
films 7.4

foreign language 6.4
hyphenated compounds 6.5
within italicized titles 5.5
italics/italic type 5.5, 7.3, 7.4
journal 6.4, 7.3, 11.2.3, 11.2.4, 11.4,
11.6
musical composition 7.4
numerical 7.4
online publications 11.2.10.1
of people 6.2
poems 7.3
quotation marks 5.5, 7.3, 7.4, 11.4
references to books 11.2.2
roman type 7.3, 7.4, 11.2.6
series 11.2.2
short 4.2, 11.3
short story 7.3
song 7.4
typeface 7.3
of writings 6.4
translators, references to 11.2.2
transliteration 3.3.2.2
truncations 2.6
type size 1.3.3
camera-ready copy 1.4.3
theses 13.4.1
typeface 1.3.2.1, 1.3.3
camera-ready copy 1.4.3.2
serif 1.3.2.1
thesis 13.4.1
titles 7.3
typescript 1.1
checking 1.2.3, 13.4.3, 15
notes 10.3
thesis 13.4
see also final version
typesetters 1.3.1, 1.3.3
comments for 1.3.2.2
editor's instructions 1.3.1
text formatting 1.3.9
typesetting by authors 1.4, 1.5
typewriters, copy production 1.3.15
typing conventions 1.3.9
typographic style for camera-ready copy
1.4.3.2

underlining 1.3.3
Universal Resource Locator (URL)
11.2.10.1, 11.2.10.2
universities

American 11.2.6
    local regulations for dissertations/
    theses 13.1, 13.2, 13.3.10, 13.4.6, 13.5
usage 2

verse quotations
    long 9.4
    omissions from 9.6
    from plays 9.6
    short 9.3
    see also poems
volume numbers
    books 8.3
    journals 11.2.4
    parentheses 11.2.2
    references 11.2.2
    roman 6.7, 11.2.2
    theses 13.3.1
volumes, publication dates 11.2.2

weights and measures 8.5
word breaks in camera-ready copy 1.4.3.2
word processors 1.1
    digital submission 1.4.2
    dissertations 13.1
    file conversion 1.3.1
    footnote function 13.3.7
    headings 13.4.2
    quotation marks 1.3.6
    special character sets 1.3.10
    theses 13.1
words definitions 9.1
World Wide Web 11.2.10.1

*The Year's Work in Modern Language
    Studies* 1.2.1, 3.3.2.2
    abbreviations 11.6

Lightning Source UK Ltd.
Milton Keynes UK
16 September 2009

143784UK00001B/56/P